UNIVERSITY OF TEXAS PRESS, *Austin*

TEXAS MOUNTAINS

Photographs by LAURENCE PARENT   *Text by* JOE NICK PATOSKI

Page 1
SIERRA DIABLO
Claret cup cactus

Frontispiece
FRANKLIN MOUNTAINS
North Franklin Peak

DEAD HORSE MOUNTAINS
Big Bend National Park

LIBRARY OF CONGRESS
CATALOGING-IN-PUBLICATION DATA

Parent, Laurence
    Texas mountains / photographs by Laurence
Parent ; text by Joe Nick Patoski.— 1st ed.
        p.   cm.
    ISBN 0-292-76592-4 (alk. paper)
    1. Mountains—Texas—Pictorial works.
2. Texas—Pictorial works. 3. Texas—Description and travel. 4. Texas—Geography. 5. Natural history—Texas—Pictorial works. 6. Landscape—Texas—Pictorial works. I. Patoski, Joe
Nick, 1951–   II. Title.

F392.A16 P37 2001
917.64′0022′2—dc21
                                              2001027434

In memory of my father, Hiram Parent,
who loved the Guadalupe Mountains
                                                    —L.P.

To my father, Victor,
who showed me Far West Texas,
and to Kris, Jake, and Andy
for putting up with me —J.N.P.

GUADALUPE MOUNTAINS
Guadalupe Mountains National Park
McKittrick Canyon

*M*any of the places pictured in this book are privately owned.

We thank the landowners who graciously allowed us access for this project.

Sadly, many of these same landowners have been abused by trespassers, litterers, poachers, and thieves.

Please enjoy their private lands vicariously through this book.

Those ranches mentioned in the text as open to the public welcome you. Otherwise, respect private property.

SIERRA VIEJA
Coal Mine Ranch

Right
SANTIAGO MOUNTAINS
Santiago Peak

CONTENTS

ar West Texas is where the mountains are in Texas. Lots of mountains. Tall mountains. Rugged mountains. Ranges of faults, folds, intrusions, and extrusions that are rocky, rough, and formidable. Texas Mountains. Within these mountains is the Texas of dreams, where everything is larger, grander, and more mythic. The eight counties that Texas' thirty-some-odd named ranges sprawl across are bigger than entire states and some nations.

The Trans-Pecos, as the region is known, stretches for some 250 miles east to west, and extends about 200 miles north to south. It is the most sparsely populated part of the state. Save for the city of El Paso, where nearly a million people live across the river from another million and a half people in Juárez, Chihuahua, Mexico, no single town in the Texas Mountains can claim more than 7,000 residents. Wide-open spaces are not just some catchphrase here. They really do exist.

The Texas Mountains first materialize on the horizon around Del Rio, Pecos, and Fort Stockton. The easternmost ranges, the Housetop and Spencer mountains, flank U.S. Highway 90 twenty miles east of Marathon like sentinels. The Glass Mountains, the first range of significant height and breadth, swell up more than a mile above sea level between Marathon, Fort Stockton, and Alpine. From there all the way to the state and international boundaries to the northwest, west, and southwest, mountains dominate the landscape.

The ranges generally run in a northwest-to-southeast line, but there is nothing else typical about them. Some consider the Texas Mountains to be the southern extension of the Rocky Mountains tumbling out of New Mexico and Colorado, although many mountain people dispute this point; only the Davis Mountains, the wettest range and one of the highest in the state, and the Guadalupes, the highest range of all, with the four tallest peaks in Texas, resemble the Rockies.

No one argues about the Texas Mountains' being the link between the Rockies and the Sierra Madre of Mexico, which rises from the desert floor almost immediately across the Rio Grande.

The other Texas Mountains are mostly fault-block ranges separated by broad basins—part of the Basin and Range Province that extends all the way from Far West Texas to the West Coast of the United States. Numerous ranges in the Big Bend, where the Rio Grande takes a long detour around several significant massifs, are igneous in origin, formed by volcanic activity far more violent than eruptions that have occurred over the last 30,000 years.

The Guadalupes, portions of the Delaware Mountains to the southeast, and the Glass Mountains, the state's easternmost major range, are part of a shoreline reef formed 280 million to 230 million years ago, before the Permian Sea receded and the reefs were thrust skyward.

Although there are many named mountains found all over the state, from the Caprock and the Cross Plains to the Big Country and the Hill Country and as far east as the Piney Woods, none are in fact mountain mountains, like the ranges in the Trans-Pecos. All the others lack sufficient height and range length to qualify as the real deal.

CHISOS MOUNTAINS
View of Big Bend National Park
from the Christmas Mountains

WYLIE MOUNTAINS
Last light

But even the Trans-Pecos Texas Mountains tend to be misunderstood. There are two Cathedral Mountains within fifty miles of each other in Brewster County—one of them 6,868 feet in elevation, a major landmark twelve miles south of Alpine, visible from Marfa and the Big Bend; the other, 6,220 feet in elevation, a major landmark on U.S. Highway 90 ten miles northwest of Marathon toward Alpine. A third Cathedral—Cathedral Peak, some 4,400 feet above sea level—is one county over, in Presidio County, southwest of Marfa. I've counted several Big Hills, Goat Mountains, a Smuggler's Gap and a Smuggler's Pass, one Blue Mountain, and one Old Blue Mountain.

A large part of this misunderstanding can be attributed to the fact that unlike most things Texan, the Texas Mountains are neither the largest nor the grandest by most standards of measurement. In the context of the western United States, the Texas Mountains are sort of puny, even. Guadalupe Peak, the highest mountain in the state at 8,749 feet, would hardly rate a glance on the other side of the New Mexico line. Arizona, Colorado, Wyoming, Montana, Hawaii—all can claim taller pinnacles. The ridges of the Sierra del Carmen in Mexico directly across from Big Bend National Park are a good 1,000 feet higher than the Chisos range, high enough to support a coniferous forest and a healthy community of black bear.

Since the Texas Mountains are so isolated from Texas' population centers and not easy to get to, not too many people know about them. Even though Interstate Highway 10 cuts through several ranges, the vast majority of travelers keep their eyes focused on the road and have no idea what they're passing through. The two most impressive ranges in the state, the Guadalupes and the Chisos, are protected as national parks, but most of the other ranges in the Trans-Pecos and the Big Bend remain unknown and unseen because they're off-limits. Unlike other western states, where federal lands sometimes account for more than half of a given state's land area, Texas, mountains included, is more than 90 percent private property.

DAVIS MOUNTAINS
Bigtooth maples

Right
DAVIS MOUNTAINS
Nature Conservancy preserve
Ponderosa pines

GLASS MOUNTAINS
Windmill

Facing page
DELAWARE MOUNTAINS
View of Guadalupe Mountains

Artifacts of some of mankind's futile efforts to conquer the Texas mountain country litter Far West Texas, in the forms of crumbling shacks, shuttered houses, downed fences, ruins of forts and roadside attractions that couldn't attract, fallow fields, and rusting machinery—all mute testimony to the truth that no matter how hard you try, sometimes it isn't enough. This land will hurt you if you're not careful. It is with a kind of twisted provincial pride that locals like to point out that practically every living plant or animal that thrives in these parts will either stick, cut, bite, or sting, just to remind you how mean this land can be.

The extreme climate is definitely a contributing factor. A tough hide and sufficient resilience to adapt to quickly changing conditions are mandatory. This is terrible dry country. Annual rainfall averages only about ten inches a year. At the close of the twentieth century a severe drought had persisted for almost a decade. Each of the four seasons has its own hellish peculiarity. The blistering winds of early spring are particularly brutal, often stirring enough dust to require wipers when driving. According to a woman from Santa Fe, New Mexico, whom I'd met on a raft trip in the Big Bend, the wind that blows through the Texas Mountains is very bad for the liver. An ovenlike heat can set in as early as March, which also may be bad for the liver. The soothing midsummer monsoons of July, August, and September that can green up the countryside overnight can bring killer floods with them, too.

When the monsoons don't come, a more and more frequent occurrence in recent

BOFECILLOS MOUNTAINS
Big Bend Ranch State Park
Volcanic tuff

years, the furnace effect down on the desert floor of the Big Bend becomes so severe that every living thing, it seems, either burns, dies, or withers away.

But even when that kind of heat is on, up on the Marfa Highlands or in the Davises and the Guadalupes, it's chilly enough at night to sleep with a blanket. The coolest summer nights in Texas are in the Texas Mountains. The heat typically subsides with the sudden arrival of a cool front, which is a distinct possibility anytime after the first of September, though the average annual first freeze doesn't come until mid-November.

Blue northers blast in the bitterest cold, dropping temperatures as much as fifty degrees in as little as an hour and occasionally leaving a dusting of snow on the mountaintops, stirring visions of the Rockies or the Alps, if only for a day or two. But even in February, temperatures are just as likely to rise to the century mark and beyond down on the lower desert as they are to plunge below the freezing mark.

Such realities are really blessings that have kept people away. Why blow the perception and have to share the stands of quaking aspen found in the Davis range, the maples of the Guadalupes and the Sierra Vieja, and the small slivers of greened-up high country that flourish on the mountaintops and in crevices and crannies, far from public view? If you're blowing through at 70 miles per hour on the interstate or peering out the window of a jet plane at 30,000 feet, you won't get it. Those of us who do get it like that just fine. We know there is much more than meets the eye at first glance. These mountains just require a little more patience and a whole lot more effort.

Geologists have been in on the secret for a long time. They come from around the world to study the rocks here and measure earth time. The ranges they examine—the Guadalupes, the Delawares, the Huecos, and the Franklins—are largely devoid of vegetative cover because of a historic dearth of moisture and are so brazen in their nakedness that they expose thousands and millions of years in their layers and folds. Elsewhere in the Texas Mountains are geological features and formations found nowhere else on the planet, a stone freak show of weird globs, jagged spires, gravity-defying balancing acts, marbled swirls, scoops of melted ice cream, and dribbled sandcastles that vary wildly from extraterrestrial to lunar in appearance.

Biologists are similarly aware of the uniqueness. Texas's mountains are all within the Chihuahuan Desert, the largest and highest desert on the continent. That not only attracts the attention of researchers, it has triggered a property-rights movement in the Texas Mountains formed by landowners frightened that rare birds, bugs, and plants will bring government agents to impose onerous restrictions that will keep them from using their property as they see fit.

If the Texas Mountains don't exactly fit into the Ansel Adams definition of majestic, they're breathtaking taken on their own terms. Texas Mountains are deceptive that way. For all their apparent desolation, life flourishes up on a remote, cloud-catching ridgeline or under a rare canopy of shade in hidden canyons fed by springs and waterfalls.

The views are bigger from the top of the Texas Mountains. On a clear day, you can easily see one hundred miles. From the top of Mount Livermore in the Davis Mountains, the highest peak in the second-highest range in Texas, mountain landmarks are clearly visible in every direction: the rectangular hump of Chinati Peak to the south; the long ridgeline of the Sierra Vieja bulging out of the flats to the south and toward the west, fading into the Van Horns, the Apaches, the Eagles, the Beaches, the Baylors, and the Sierra Diablo. Beyond them all is the lone sentinel of Sierra Blanca, marking the route to El Paso and the Pacific. And when the winds are calm and the light is sharp, the Guadalupes hurtle toward the heavens from the northern horizon.

No other North American mountain range can claim such a geologically significant site as the roadside park on U.S. Highway 385 south of Marathon. The historical marker there identifies Los Caballos, the Dead Horse Mountains. These grassy desert hills with outcroppings of limestone blocks breaking out of their sloped surface here and there mark the spot where east meets west, continentally speaking. The limestone blocks are the westernmost pieces of the Ouachita Fold Belt, an ancient range that is mostly below the surface of the land mass that is connected to the mountains of eastern North America, specifically the Ozark and Appalachian ranges. The grassy slopes are the tail end of the younger Rockies.

Humans have a deep history in these mountains. Occupation by small bands of hunters and gatherers has been traced back as far as 12,000 years in the Trans-Pecos and Big Bend. For these nomadic peoples, the Texas Mountains were a far easier place to subsist in than, say, Aspen or Sun Valley, at least back then. The desert provided a bounty of foods, medicines, fiber, and building material, with abundant wildlife supplementing the vegetative resources.

The Texas Mountains were on the historic transit routes linking indigenous peoples traveling between present-day Mexico and New Mexico. They sheltered way stations on the paths taken by Spanish explorers who came into this part of the New World in search of riches, beginning in 1521 at La Junta de los Ríos, the junction where the Río Conchos joins the Rio Grande above present-day Presidio. The river valley is the oldest continuously cultivated farmland in North America.

Missionaries, raiders, soldiers, and prospectors were followed by a trickle of pioneers, miners, ranchers, farmers, promoters, dreamers, and robbers, first from the south and then from the east, on foot, on horseback, by stagecoach, rail, highway, river, and air. Today, the major southern transcontinental rail and road routes connecting the East Coast with the West skirt around and between the Davis, Wylie, Apache, Carrizo, Baylor, Beach, Sierra Diablo, Eagle, Quitman, Malone, and Franklin ranges.

The few people who do live around these mountains all seem to be born storytellers, and more often than not their story lines will convey a sense of place that pretty much sums up why they live where they live and do what they do. It's different out here.

Far away. Wild. Primitive. Rough.

Sounds horrible. But almost every resident telling you that will also tell you that's pretty much just the way they like it. The attitude has instilled in them the same mythic qualities that permeate the land. I've met more than a few folks who I'm convinced could lasso a tornado just like Pecos Bill did, if they ever set their minds to it. All that wide-open space works wonders with the imagination.

Listen to them long enough, and you'll understand why they consider it such a privilege to live in this isolated pocket of magnificence tucked away in the far distant corner of

DAVIS MOUNTAINS
Scarlet bouvardia, yuccas, and
prickly pear cactus

CHISOS MOUNTAINS
Big Bend National Park
South Rim

a state where superlatives are the norm. It ain't easy, they'll tell you, but they wouldn't trade it for all the riches in the outside world.

Photographer Laurence Parent and I both had reservations about doing a book on such a remarkable place. Despite all the remoteness and discouraging features of the Texas Mountains, the outside world is encroaching fast enough without our help. Everyone, it seems, has a plan in mind for these mountains, and not all of those plans are good.

The Texas Mountains are where New York City spreads its sewage sludge, where Texas, Vermont, and New Hampshire were going to bury their collective nuclear waste under the topsoil, thereby lowering the risk of killing people should any radiation leak out, since hardly anyone lives in the Texas Mountains, or so the thinking goes.

The Texas Mountains crowd a border that is futilely fenced and patrolled. Its ridges have become prime real estate for television and radio antennae, cellular telephone towers, microwave relay stations, giant radars to scan the skies for drug smugglers, and giant propellers to generate "clean" energy (Texas and North Dakota are considered the top two states for developing wind power in the twenty-first century).

The valleys between the mountains have been designated ideal environments for military pilots from the United States and Germany to practice low-level training missions by buzzing the vast cattle ranches that epitomize so much of the region's culture and traditions.

Our misgivings were outweighed by our love and appreciation for this place that others describe as godforsaken. We know our subject well. Laurence has more titles relating to these mountains on the bookshelves of the Panther Junction headquarters of Big Bend National Park than any other photographer or writer. And in more than twenty-five years of writing for *Texas Monthly* magazine and other publications, I've devoted more

DAVIS MOUNTAINS
Milk vetch

Right
BEACH MOUNTAINS
Hackberry Creek

EAGLE MOUNTAINS
View from summit

column inches to these mountains and the people in them than to any other region of the state. It's Laurence's favorite part of Texas, and it's my favorite place too.

I got hooked at the age of six, when I climbed to the top of the small hill adjacent to the Chisos Mountains Lodge in Big Bend National Park, rode on horseback to the Window and peered out over what seemed then to be the end of the world, and, at a time when I still believed in Santa Claus, fixated on the idea that there was actually a place called the Christmas Mountains. The relationship continued through my youth, when I discovered there isn't a more enchanted city view in Texas than the twinkling lights of El Paso and Juárez beheld at night from Scenic Drive in the Franklins. I learned firsthand of the connection between the people of the Texas Mountains and the mountains themselves by climbing the pilgrims' path to the top of Mount Cristo Rey and straddling the boundary between Texas, New Mexico, and Chihuahua. As an adult, I've touched the roof of Texas atop Guadalupe Peak, perched on the edge of the South Rim of the Chisos in Big Bend, and watched a comet from the top of Mount Locke at McDonald Observatory, illuminated by more stars than the eye can comprehend, in the darkest skies in America. I've seen more than I could have ever hoped for in the process of writing this book.

The last time I was in the Chisos Basin, I noticed that little hill by the lodge again. Forty-three years had passed since I first scaled it. For much of that time, the little hill didn't seem that big. It was but another example of how things shrink and diminish when you grow up. Lately, though, it's started looking more like a mountain to me again, just like it did when I was a kid. Just like it does to kids scurrying up its rocks today, I bet.

GUADALUPE MOUNTAINS
Guadalupe Mountains National Park
Hunter Peak, high country forest below peak

You know you're in Far West Texas when the handshakes are firm, no matter if it's a man or a woman doing the shaking, when drivers of vehicles passing in the other direction lift a finger off the steering wheel—the Hidy sign—as a form of greeting no matter where you are, and you see mountains no matter where you look.

A brief geology lesson, as taught by Dr. Phil Goodell, professor of geology at the University of Texas at El Paso:

> This is a basin and range province. That's a physiographic characteristic of our region. But to really understand, you've got to think about plate tectonics. All the mountain ranges in Texas can be attributed to the ripping apart of the earth. We call this the Rio Grande Rift. Vulcanism was the precursor of this rifting. West of the Pecos River, land starts rising, all the way to Chihuahua, Arizona, and Nevada. The crust of the earth's been fractured, faulted, blown out by two different types of volcanic activity, bulging up and stretching apart.
>
> The Quitmans and the Eagles—these are calderas. They were big mothers and they blew off violently. The Chinatis, the Davises—they're calderas, too, formed by huge, violent eruptions, thirty, thirty-five million years ago. And then there's the black ooze kind of vulcanism. That's different. You don't see too much of that on mountaintops. But there are one hundred of them sitting in the Rio Grande Rift throughout West Texas into New Mexico. There's a little bit of basalt flow too on I-10 from El Paso to the Quitmans. The Sierra Vieja—that's one of your outflow facies. It's the Mitchell Mesa Tuft outflow from the Chinatis.

MARATHON is the first town in the Texas Mountains that westbound travelers on U.S. Highway 90 encounter. It's the home of the Gage Hotel, a splendid railroad hotel designed by Henry Trost, the most distinguished architect of the great Southwest, and built by rancher Alfred Gage.

The hotel and the town had all but blown away with the wind by 1978 when a Houston couple, J. P. and Mary Jon Bryan, bought the place and restored it to attract travelers headed to Big Bend National Park, sixty miles south. The Bryans did a makeover of the hotel's restaurant, too, and the Cafe Cenizo and its New Southwest cuisine menu quickly established a reputation as the Trans-Pecos's first fine-dining establishment, ushering in the modern age of tourism in the Texas Mountains and creating stars like chef Grady Spears of Alpine, who elevated chuck-wagon campfire fare to highfalutin cowboy cuisine. Twenty years after the Bryans began their makeover, the town of 800 sports several bed-and-breakfasts, art galleries, cafes, and stores, all catering to folks passing through. Unlike most other small towns in Texas, Marathon is on the grow again.

QUITMAN MOUNTAINS
Malone and Finlay mountains in distance

FIELD NOTES—*Glass Mountains. From U.S. Highway 67 between Fort Stockton and Alpine, the Glass Mountains gradually swell above the plain, eventually becoming real mountains, albeit minus mountainlike vegetation. The pinnacles and ridges hide a relict forest, a remnant of wetter times, within the folds of the upper slopes, and a six-sided stone castle once featured in* Town and Country, *a magazine dedicated to gracious living. Elk, wiped out by hunters early in the twentieth century, were reintroduced by a rancher during the 1970s and now thrive alongside an abundant population of mule deer.*

Shadowing the range from the road, a prominent southeast-northwest spine called Old Blue Mountain that is an extension of the Ouachita Fold Belt, which has been essentially buried under the surface all the way from Arkansas to here, suddenly leaps out off the plain to arch over the main northeast-southwest ridge. East meets west at this surreal crossroads.

From here, the Glasses appear practically untouched by humans, an impression betrayed by their abuse, says Dr. D. J. Sibley, who grew up around the Glass range and built the castle in the high country. "Obviously, there is a great deal of seemingly vacant land that was overused by ranchers until they almost destroyed the capacity to grow grass. Sheep raisers so greatly reduced the grass that brush took over the country, which has been true over most of the Texas ranchlands. There was no such thing as a mesquite tree beyond the Pecos River a century ago."

The slate-gray slopes of the Glass range make an ideal canvas for the ongoing light show that plays until the sun drops below the horizon, especially in the southwestern extreme of the range where it reaches its highest point at Cathedral Mountain, 6,220 feet above sea level, a beacon between Marathon and Alpine.

Five miles across a small valley and U.S. Highway 90 and the Southern Pacific rail line is another range, the Del Nortes, and Mount Ord, 6,803 feet above sea level, whose north-facing slopes are almost dense with dark green splotches of juniper and yucca. Framed by the peaks of the Glasses rising to the east and the radio tower on top, the mountain exudes a slight aura of grandiosity.

A marker at a roadside park six miles east of Alpine identifies this as the Ancient Rocks Boundary—the Glass Mountains to the east being limestone reefs deposited in the Cretaceous and Permian seas about 135 million and 250 million years ago, respectively, overlying deformed rocks in the Ouachita Fold Belt (such as Old Blue Mountain); the mountains to the west, northwest, and southwest being layers of lava and associated leftovers from vulcanism of 25 million to 35 million years ago, blown upward, into, and over most sedimentary rock.

FIELD NOTES—*Ten miles south of Marathon. The Los Caballos (Spanish shorthand for the Dead Horse Mountains) historical marker by a roadside park takes note of the low range running up from the east-northeast peppered with outcroppings of hard rock breaking through the high desert grassland, surrounded by small peaks and hills—where the Rockies meet the Appalachians. Nowhere but Texas.*

GLASS MOUNTAINS
View of Iron Mountain
from flanks of Gilliland Peak

DEAD HORSE MOUNTAINS
Black Gap Wildlife Management Area

Thirty-two miles west of Marathon is Alpine, a ranching community that has evolved into the commercial center of the Trans-Pecos and happens to be right in the thick of this mountains crossroads. Jagged peaks, smooth cones, rugged outcroppings, fields of giant boulders, and soaring ridges surround the town, with the Davis and Chinati ranges dominating the western horizon.

"It's quite a view," Mimi Dopson smiles at the top of Hancock Hill, four hundred feet above the campus of Sul Ross State University in Alpine, as her husband, Robert, huffs and puffs to catch up. From here, they can see the West of the imagination, a broad range thick with cattle, deer, and antelope, and mountains everywhere.

The Dopsons are fiftysomething urban refugees from Austin who've reinvented their lives in the Texas Mountains. He's a retired dentist, she was his office manager. Both are students now at Sul Ross and avid ceramists, who stay active hiking, biking, and swimming three times a week at Balmorhea, one of the world's largest outdoor swimming pools and a literal oasis in the desert.

Climbing Hancock Hill to the school desk up on top is part of their regimen. Jim Kitchen, a student at Sul Ross in the 1970s, built the trail, then snitched the desk out of one of the buildings and with help hauled it up the hill. I sign the log in a drawer of the desk and write some comments about the inspirational view, as is the custom.

"We think we're in paradise," says Mimi Dopson. They are not alone. People like Robert James Waller, an author from the Midwest who wrote the best-selling novel *The Bridges of Madison County* and relocated to a nearby ranch in 1992, and Doyle Bramhall, a blues composer and collaborator with the late Stevie Ray Vaughan, both spent their royalties to buy land in the area.

In spite of the influx of newcomers who have pushed the population beyond 6,000, the town has managed to retain its character and quirks, the latter best appreciated at Kokernot Field, built by Herbert Kokernot Jr. of the 06 Ranch in the 1940s for the local semipro baseball team; it's a miniature of Yankee Stadium, only far more pleasing to the eye.

A defining moment in the town's history came during the 1980s when local merchants fought off a Wal-Mart, making Alpine the first town in Texas to do so (one must drive to Fort Stockton, sixty miles away, for such conveniences). Still, westbound travelers

GLASS MOUNTAINS
Iron Mountain pond

DEAD HORSE MOUNTAINS
Big Bend National Park, historic ore tramway
tower and view of Sierra del Carmen

entering town are greeted by an oversized pair of golden arches that make sure no one misses the local McDonald's.

From another overlook south of town on State Highway 118, the illuminated arches and all of Alpine are lost in a vast sea of highland grasses and diminished by the mountains ringing the town—Mount Ord, Ranger Peak, Twin Peaks, Paisano Peak, Mitre Peak, George Washington Mountain—some rises contoured by wind and water for millions of years, others of volcanic origin still reeking of the violence that made them, events that transpired long before mammals appeared on earth. In that context, man's presence is insignificant, a gnat on the windshield of time. McDonald's doesn't even exist.

"One day in August 1995 my husband, Jim, and I stood on our land south of Alpine, looked toward the southwest, and saw a smudgy haze diminishing Cathedral Mountain to an outline," says Fran Sage, explaining why she cofounded a Sierra Club group in the Big Bend.

The builder was less than two months away from completing our house for the perfect retirement in what we considered paradise—and we see polluted air blocking the view in an area with few cars and no industry, coming from East Texas and from Mexico, especially the Carbon I and II plants across from Eagle Pass, Texas, near Piedras Negras, Coahuila, Mexico.

Realizing that such a remote region as ours is not free of dirty air, and that decisions affecting our health and our vistas were being made in Austin, Washington, D.C., and Mexico, Jim and I made a phone call in April 1996 to the Lone Star chapter of the Sierra Club. That led to the founding of a Sierra Club group in the Big Bend. We'd been advised against it out here, told that the Big Bend is ranching country, that many citizens are hostile to environmentalists and their organizations. We were even told it would be dangerous. The predictions were wrong. We started with thirty-one members, eight of whom came to the organizational meeting at our house. In four years membership has grown to over

GLASS MOUNTAINS
Iron Mountain and distant Gilliland Peak

Facing page
GLASS MOUNTAINS
Gilliland Peak

one hundred. We have received community support fighting the disposal of radio-active waste in West Texas. We are best known for working to decrease air pollution by pressuring the Environmental Protection Agency and the Texas Natural Resource Conservation Commission. Twice those agencies have come to West Texas and heard the anger and concern. We may have helped get the BRAVO study on the sources of air pollution in Big Bend National Park under way, and are working with the Texas Department of Health studying health effects. The issues are tangled up in politics in Texas and across the border. But we're keeping up the pressure. Perhaps we'll even see the air cleaner down the line.

"WE JUST CAN'T FIND COWBOYS ANYMORE," Tom Beard tells me as a way of explaining how progress has affected ranching on tens of thousands of acres of the Leoncita Ranch in the Barrilla Mountains northeast of Alpine, which he and his wife, Val, who is also county judge of Brewster County, operate.

DEL NORTE MOUNTAINS
Cholla cactus, Woodward Agate Ranch

This is a big ranch, and it used to take eighteen or twenty cowboys for roundup. We were having more and more mavericks left out on the range, to the point it was hurting our breeding program. So we tried helicopters.

With a bunch of cowboys, you'd be able to gather cattle on maybe 5,000 acres a day. This group just did 35,000 acres. Helicopters don't stress the cattle as much. They get to the pens without a problem. With cowboys on horses, they get mad, huffing and puffing, sometimes. They're in bad shape. A helicopter doesn't bother 'em. The mamas don't have as many dogies.

We used to have a remuda of sixty horses. Now we're down to twenty. All we need is about ten people in the pens. Which means we really don't need too many extras. We save on personnel. We save on overhead. When you're working with horses, you're writing a lot of small checks. With helicopters, you write just one big check.

DEL NORTE MOUNTAINS
Calamity Creek, Woodward Agate Ranch

This is a business for me. I can't get nostalgic about it. Lot of cowboys at some ranches would rather look in the mirror than work in the pens. The business is not that great, but it's working for us. It's making money. A small operation with fifty to one hundred calves, there's no way to make it. It's just a sideline.

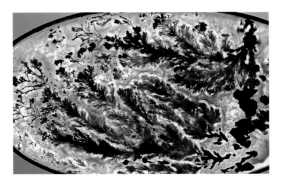

DEL NORTE MOUNTAINS
Woodward Agate Ranch
Plume agate

"THIS IS THE ONLY place in the world you can find the Texas red plume agate," says Trey Woodward, who, along with his wife, Jayson, runs the Woodward Ranch, sixteen miles south of Alpine in the Cathedral Mountains. The ranch, founded in 1884 by his great-grandfather, was one of the first in the Trans-Pecos to welcome visitors, because its rocks were far more valuable than its grazing pastures.

"More than half of the rocks pictured on the cover of *Agates of North America* come from this ranch," Woodward says. "The only precious opal in Texas comes off the top of that hill over there. We have full hookups, showers, rest rooms. We charge fifty cents a pound for the good rocks you find. We put on a gem show in Alpine every April, and every Memorial Day weekend Sunday, we put on the Rockhound Barbecue and Roundup."

In 1993, an earthquake measuring 3.3 on the Richter scale knocked off a piece of Cathedral Peak, which the Woodward Ranch overlooks. "A pillar about twelve feet high and seven feet in diameter vibrated loose and fell down," Woodward says. "I also had a twenty-four-point set of antlers that my grandfather killed. It was the largest deer killed in Brewster County that year. That rack fell off the wall and broke one side from the earthquake."

Although motorized transportation has improved mobility, the country around the Woodward and in all of Far West Texas is still isolated territory. "My granddad used to tell me it took 'em a week to go from the mines at Terlingua to Alpine in two twenty-mule teams," Woodward told me. "We're still on microwave telephone. We only get 1500 baud. We can't get on the World Wide Web. We can E-mail, though. A census taker told our commissioner that people out here in this part of the state are statistically insignificant."

FIELD NOTES—*Sierra del Carmen. In May 2000 one of the biggest wildfires in the history of the state broke out on the Cook Ranch in the Glass Mountains, scorching 47,000 acres. Among those fighting the fire were the Diablos, men from three Mexican villages on the Rio Grande in the Sierra del Carmen. The Diablos were trained as firefighters by rangers at Big Bend National Park, their neighbors across the river, as part of a program started in 1990 by the National Park Service and SUDUE, the Park Service's Mexican counterpart.*

"We're not in the middle of nowhere, but you can actually see it from here," says John Morlock, fire management officer at Big Bend National Park, explaining why it made sense to train forty-five villagers from Boquillas, San Vicente, and Santa Elena. Those communities rely on two stores in the park for milk, *un seis-pack*, and other basics, since Muzquiz, the closest trading center in Mexico, is 150 miles and a ten-hour bus ride south. If a fire broke out in an isolated area of the park, officials could rely on the Diablos to assist.

For most Diablos, the Glass Mountains fire marked the first time they'd ventured into the United States beyond the national park.

"They were really proud, very professional, and well organized," says Derek Ammons, a Big Bend lead forestry technician, who fought alongside them. "After we'd get off the

SIERRA DEL CARMEN AND DEAD HORSE MOUNTAINS
Big Bend National Park, Boquillas Canyon

line, they continued wearing their hard hats with chin straps still on and their Nomex shirts around the motel."

They were good—so good that when the entire American West seemed to erupt in flames later that summer, the Diablos were called again. In July a crew helped battle the Peek fire in eastern Arizona, followed by a second team that fought fires on the Ute Mountain reservation and at the Mesa Verde National Park in Colorado. On September 6 a third crew went to work on a large grass fire in the Texas Hill Country near Kerrville.

Paid the standard $10.68 an hour wage for their two-week stints, some returned to their villages with the equivalent of three years' income for three weeks' work, while their reputation as exceptionally fierce combatants grew larger.

"They can take us as far as they want," Gerardo "Jerry" Ureste Romero says without emotion, sitting on a bare mattress on the shaded patio of his small adobe home in Boquillas next to his brother, José Angel Romero, or "Charlie," while his wife sweeps the dirt floor nearby. "We know it's dangerous, but we're not afraid. If we were, we wouldn't be going."

"There wasn't any fear," reported Gabriel Ureste Padilla, 29, while resting under a mesquite canopy on the Texas bank of the muddy river, freshly returned from a firefight in Colorado. He did notice, though, that there were *"pocos indios,"* hardly any Indians like himself.

"The Diablos are extremely physically fit," John Morlock says. "After all, they're desert-hard people who've been living outdoors all their lives." But there were certain adjustments to make. "We took men who'd never spent a night in a motel, fed them three meals a day of American food. They'd ask, 'Why are we eating so early? Why are we eating so much?' They weren't used to the food. At first, they hardly ate anything because it was so different. The lights of Albuquerque blew them away when we were returning from Colorado. The bus climbed over a rise, and all at once they did a big 'Ahhhhhh.' None had ever flown before, and in Colorado they were going to work in helicopters. By the fourth day, they were taking pictures and waving."

FIELD NOTES—*State Highway 118 southbound from Alpine. A drive south from Marathon, Alpine, or Marfa toward the Rio Grande leaves behind grasslands that are a cattleman's ideal and descends into the devil's playground of dry rubble tossed out by volcanic eruptions, thick layers of ancient lava crust oozed out of vents, worn away sea bottoms, sudden upthrusts squeezed out from colliding continents like so many pimples.*

The intensity builds with each passing landmark: Cienega and Cathedral, the groaning flattop of Elephant Mountain, a semi-monolith like an elephant out of proportion with the rest of the landscape, the classic lines of Agua Fria Mountain, the stark nobility of Santiago Mountain rising above a treeless plain, the exposed western flank of Packsaddle Mountain deftly sliced away by the Creator's Ginsu knife, the melting ice cream cone called Hen Egg Peak, the naked Rosillos and Christmas ranges. This is the despoblado, *the uninhabited place, as the Spanish described it. I feel like I've fallen off the edge of the earth.*

At the end of the drop is the massif of the mighty Chisos, ethereal and majestic, flanked by Santa Elena Canyon to the west and the banded high ridge wall of the Sierra del Carmen to the east, levitating above the desert flats.

ROSILLOS MOUNTAINS

34

SANTIAGO MOUNTAINS
Prickly pear cacti and yuccas

John Klingemann, the curator of exhibits and public programs at the Museum of the Big Bend in Alpine, knows the route "like the back of my hand." A 1992 graduate of Alpine High School, he survived what until recently was the longest school bus commute in the United States, the 160-mile round-trip from Terlingua to Alpine.

On a typical day, I'd wake up at 4:30, and after getting dressed, go into the kitchen and have a breakfast of either *huevos rancheros* or eggs sunny-side up with bacon, depending on who had cooked. My mother was from Mexico and my father a man of German descent from Texas.

By 5:20, I was driven to the public school, where the old bus awaited us. It looked like a spaceship in the distance with its sidelights lit. Some people would be standing outside or in their vehicles trying to catch a radio station from far away so they could keep up with the latest music. Others would already be on the bus, asleep or talking. The older you were, the farther back on the bus you got to sit. If you were a senior you could have two seats to yourself where you could stretch your legs across and sleep somewhat comfortably. The youngest always had to sit at the front, two to a seat. After a while the bus driver would honk the horn and we would all file in.

The first landmark was Bee Mountain. It sort of resembled the letter *B* on its side, but others told me it was called that because of the bees found in its crevices. Sleeping on the bus took some getting used to. Several times we would hit bumps on the road and you would fly a couple of feet in the air and crash back into your

DEL NORTE MOUNTAINS
Woodward Agate Ranch

seat. It was usually dark when we arrived in Alpine, but at certain times of the year on the 02 Flats, you could see a beautiful sunrise. Santiago Peak was on the 02 Flats, and it always looked beautiful with the sunset behind it. I always imagined living in a castle on top of the peak.

We were usually awakened by the time we got to the big hill outside of Alpine because it was so steep that you would roll out of your seat. Around 7:30, we arrived at the high school. Most of us would hang out in the gym or outside, waiting for classes to begin.

After school we boarded the bus and headed home. On the way back, I always looked forward to Cathedral Mountain, which indeed did look like a cathedral. Cienega Mountain was a sign we were close to the Border Patrol station. Elephant Mountain always let me know that we were about to hit the 02 Flats, where the environment changed. It was like an opening to another world.

Right after the 02 Flats came Luna Vista, an old adobe beer joint on the side of Adobe Walls Mountain that still stood strong. Off to the right you could see Packsaddle, Hen Egg, and Agua Fria mountains. Then came the Christmas Mountains and Wildhorse Mountain, where some of my friends lived. Willow Mountain reminded me of the mountain in *Close Encounters of the Third Kind.* It had the appearance of a mountain that someone had taken a fork to and scraped the sides. Finally came Bee Mountain. I knew I was home.

I made friends on that bus who will be my friends for the rest of my life.

CHRISTMAS MOUNTAINS
Willow Mountain

ROSILLOS MOUNTAINS
From Grapevine Hills

Often on the way back we did our homework because there was nothing else to do. I read quite a bit. By the time I got to college I had read many of the required readings for freshman- and sophomore-level classes. We would play card games or, if we were lucky and had a bus with a tape deck, we would listen to music.

Sometimes we played jokes on each other to pass the time. If one of the guys was lying down, the rest of us would dog-pile him in his seat. We always dropped people off along the road at different ranches, so our numbers would thin out by the time we reached Terlingua.

The only time that I did not ride the bus to Alpine was when I played football my senior year. I stayed in town with one of my friends and had the luxury of waking up at 7:30 in the morning. My teammates were always amazed at how happy and energized I was. They never knew how lucky they had it.

TERLINGUA HAS ITS OWN high school now. The greater Terlingua–Study Butte metropolitan area, a six-mile scattering of civilization hugging the road from the intersection of State Highway 118, the western gateway to the national park, to Terlingua along Farm Road 170, is on a growth spurt. Even the old ghost town, once the site of a mercury mine and a prosperous community of several thousand until the mercury quit and the mine closed in the late 1940s, has been reborn as the cultural hub of south Brewster County.

CHRISTMAS MOUNTAINS
Corazones Peaks

Facing page
BOFECILLOS MOUNTAINS AND SIERRA RICA
Big Bend Ranch State Park, Colorado Canyon

BULLIS GAP RANGE
Rio Grande, Lower Canyons

Previous pages
SANTIAGO MOUNTAINS
Santiago Peak

It started with the first Terlingua International Chili Cookoff in 1967, an excuse for city folks to dress up like Gabby Hayes and go loco on the desert while comparing their skills at preparing a bowl o' red, the official state dish of Texas. The event, staged on the first Saturday in November, has split into two competing international championship cookoffs, conducted simultaneously five miles apart (even federal judge Lucius Bunton couldn't resolve the groups' differences), that draw 10,000 chiliheads from around the world.

Since 1990, a water supply company, a regional medical clinic, and a radio station, KYOTE 100.1-FM, have materialized, joining the high school as points of interest. The Lajitas Desert Challenge and Mountain Bike Festival in February is beginning to rival the chili cookoffs in visitor count. The road into the ghost town from the highway has been paved. A barbecue joint called When Pigs Fly that opened in the late 1990s posts a sign out front welcoming tour buses, and the beer cooler in the Terlingua Store stocks imported beer as well as domestic.

The main attractions, the desert and the mountains, are the same as ever, drawing a crowd every afternoon to the porch of the store, where locals and visitors shoot the breeze and watch the fading sunlight play on the western face of the Chisos.

The daily gathering includes river guides from Far Flung Adventures comparing notes after a long day (or days) at the office, Elderhostel tour groups, families on vacation, hikers from the national park and the state park, a lone motorcyclist on a cross-country trek,

43

strangers from Florida, England, and every part of Texas, and twenty or so regulars who congregate at one end, two of them rolling their own cigarettes, most of them drinking a beer or three.

It is November. There's been rain on the desert, four inches in the month of October —practically half the annual rainfall—and the tourists are already drifting in for Thanksgiving. The furnace heat that defines the six months of summer on this part of the desert has vanished.

There are clouds in the sky. Fronts blowing out of the Rockies and in from the Pacific are working their way down to the river, clearing out the stagnant air that has been fouling the once-pristine skies of the Big Bend increasingly since the late 1970s. On a clear day, from the top of the South Rim in the Chisos, you can see almost two hundred miles away. Since the construction of two coal-fired power plants near Piedras Negras on the Texas-Mexico border 136 miles downriver, those days have become more and more rare. Big Bend, in the middle of the proverbial nowhere, has the worst air pollution of any national park in the western United States. The sun, lower on the horizon as autumn advances toward winter, is throwing off what Steve Fromholz describes as "Michelangelo light."

I find Fromholz, the noted Texas singer-songwriter, next door to the porch in a booth of the adobe-walled Starlight Theatre restaurant, a reconfigured remnant of the ghost town that is hands down the best restaurant in the Big Bend. Like many other residents, he too has dropped out of the city rat race, at least part-time, and augments his music career with work as a river guide for Far Flung.

Sitting next to him is Sam Richardson, who apologizes for missing sunset on the porch. He did two interpretative hiking tours earlier in the day for Elderhostel groups and was running late. Business is good, almost too good, he says, but you get it while you can.

"Today it was the national park. Tomorrow is the state park. They pay for six nights, transportation, lodging. We do the rest. Tom Gaffaney talks about literature of the Southwest; he's writing a novel right now. Ken Barnes, sitting up there at the bar, comes in to talk paleontology. He came out here in 1969 with a survey crew, became the county surveyor and taught himself all about dinosaurs. Enrique Madrid from Redford comes in to talk about the border—on this side, it's all about rules and regulations; on the other side, it's all theater. He's a scholar, he's well researched, published. He's the one who got the Marines out of the neighborhood. It's different over there with the Marines and the Border Patrol. You don't sense that over around here. Then we do a hike and talk. Ross Maxwell [the first superintendent of Big Bend National Park] said this is the world's largest geology textbook. I say it's the world's largest textbook, period."

Sam's favorite hike is the twelve-mile round-trip from the Chisos Basin in the national park up to the South Rim, the biggest, broadest panorama of earth and sky I've ever laid eyes on. You can see most of the Big Bend from Emory Peak.

"It takes you most of the day with a backpack," he says. "You can do a round-trip in a day, but I like to stay overnight up top. When you backpack up there, make camp, and sit on that rim, there's nothing like it. There isn't a prettier view. It's the whole experience. By the time you've hiked up there, had supper, you feel connected to the universe, quiet and connected. Life makes sense."

CHISOS MOUNTAINS
Big Bend National Park, Elephant Tusk

A lot of the regulars at the Starlight are trying to make sense of news that the informal crossing between the national park and the Mexican village of Boquillas has been closed. Someone from the village was evidently caught selling peyote buttons and/or other illegal drugs to a ranger, so the Park Service closed the crossing.

The village is taking a major economic hit for the transgression, since tourism is practically the only source of income. Visitors pay two dollars to ride in a rowboat across the river; another few dollars to take a burro or pickup truck into the quaint settlement, which lacks running water and electricity; and a few dollars more to eat at Falcon's, Boquillas's cafe (where three soft tacos, three burritos, beer, and soft drinks are all one dollar), drink at one of two cantinas, sleep at the Buzzard's Roost bed-and-breakfast, or buy one of the glittery rocks that are arranged on tables in front of practically every residence. Park ranger Marcos Paredes, also drinking at the Starlight bar, says he hears the crossing will open by the weekend.

"You should have been here two nights before," Sam tells me. "We had a fund-raiser auction for the radio station, raised more than $4,000. All these parkies were here. We fetched $280 for the privilege of throwing a pie in the face of Bill Wright, the head ranger. Fromholz ended up leg-wrestling on the floor for donations, men and women both. There was a lot of drinking going on, but nobody got hurt. I've never seen a fight in here. This place doesn't need bouncers.

"We're living a lot of people's dreams here. We really are. But this is a harsh way to make a living. Most of us are making wages that the government would qualify as below the poverty line. But we make out just fine."

If Terlingua is being discovered by people other than Texans who come in search of solitude and the sweet sensation of being swallowed up by the Big Bend, Sam and Steve and others are ready to welcome them.

"Frederick Jackson Turner said there's several stages of frontier development," Sam goes on. "The frontier of the conquistador explorers, the frontier of traders and trappers, the frontier of mining, the frontier of agriculture and trade, the frontier of organized government. We're in the next to last frontier, based on tourism trade. We've got a bed tax now, and a tourism board."

Angie Dean, the Starlight's owner, slides into the booth. Times are good, she says, noting that there's finally been enough rain to fill stock tanks and put a flow into the river. "It'll be a really good spring for wildflowers, for the first time in maybe ten years." Spring comes to the Big Bend in early February when the Big Bend bluebonnets, giant lupines easily twice the size of the official state wildflower, pop out. "Enjoy it while you can," she advises. Sure enough, it'll be hot and dry again sooner than you know.

Moselle Jeffrey, a woman who has built her own straw bale house, photovoltaic solar panel power generator, and partial rain catchment system, sits down next to Sam. "There's a lot of women into construction around here," she says. When she leaves, another woman, Collie Ryan, scoots into her place. She paints mandalas on hubcaps. Mandalas are wheels, based on mathematical formulas that balance colors and shapes, she explains. "It sounds simplistic, but it's not. It has a beginning and an end. It's an old symbol, as old as mankind. Cut an orange in half and it's a mandala." She sells her work in the United States and

CHISOS MOUNTAINS
Big Bend National Park, South Rim

Europe. She's a real Luddite, Sam says, paying her a Terlingua compliment as he buys a mandala. She lives without electricity or running water, on next to nothing, surviving on the desert just fine.

The after-dinner chatter drifts to folklore, which is abundant in the Big Bend, where an alligator really does roam the Rio Grande and the Marfa Lights and other ghost lights in the Chinatis and the Cienegas are fact, not fiction. Sam speaks of the devil who roamed around Presidio and Ojinaga. He lived in La Cerita de la Santa Cruz and played on a wire stretched between those mountains and the Chinatis, until a priest holding a cross tricked him and drove him into a cave there. "When the devil was having his fight with the priest, he threw a big ball into the city," Angie Dean says. "It's there in front of the library," Sam notes. Before the missionaries arrived, some say, the devil was a spider that swooped down from its web to eat children. "It's also where Pancho Villa sat in his command post in the Battle of Ojinaga in 1914 and literally kicked the Mexican *federales* into the river," Sam says, and that's no folktale. Neither is the fact that the mascot of Presidio High, directly across the river from the mountains where the priest sealed the cave, is the Blue Devil.

Chupacabra, the supernatural being that sucks blood from goats, is mentioned. So are shape-changers in the form of black dogs with wings that steal babies. "I've seen them," Angie swears. She says it so convincingly, I believe her.

"The place feeds the imagination," Sam says after Angie excuses herself. Steve Fromholz breaks into a wide grin and stretches. "Man, this is the life." I believe him, too.

> Soon after the evening meal, as I was sitting on a rock, looking into the far-away beautiful mountains in Mexico and enjoying the lovely evening shadows so typical of West Texas at dusk, my emotions were calmed and I felt peace and happiness.
>
> —HALLIE STILLWELL, IN HER AUTOBIOGRAPHY, *I'll Gather My Geese*

NO WOMAN OR MAN defined the Big Bend in the twentieth century quite like Hallie Stillwell did. She lived ninety-nine years, most of it in the wild country, and passed away in 1997. When she taught school in Presidio, she kept a pistol in her desk as a last line of defense if Pancho Villa happened to cross the river on a raid. She was mistress of the 22,000-acre Stillwell Ranch near Heath Canyon, northeast of the national park and forty-six miles southeast of Marathon, for eighty years, running it on her own for almost fifty years after her husband, Roy, died. She was a newspaper columnist, the Brewster County justice of the peace, a sharpshooter, and beginning in 1969, the proprietor of the Stillwell Store and R.V. Park, six miles north of the national park, the put-in point for raft trips down the Lower Canyons of the Rio Grande, a six-day-minimum float on one of the most secluded stretches of waterway on the continent.

The best hot shower I've ever taken in my life was at the Stillwell Store, following a raft trip through Boquillas Canyon for five days, and I got to shake Miss Hallie's hand too. Even then, she was larger than life. She's gone now, but Hallie's Hall of Fame Museum next to the store and the RV park bring her back to life.

Facing page
CHISOS MOUNTAINS
Big Bend National Park
Seasonal waterfall

49

Bill Bourbon is a geologist, firefighter, and guide who has lived in south Brewster County for the past thirty years. He once showed me a petrified forest near Old Ore Road in the national park, the exact location of which I'm sworn never to reveal. The home he shares with his wife, Sarah, who is sales manager of the Big Bend Natural History Association in the national park, is on a mesa that looks out on the Chisos and the Christmas mountains, a million-dollar view if I've ever seen one.

> My father was a traveling salesman whose route took him to the far reaches of West Texas. My older brother was the first to accompany him on his summer trips to Alpine and surrounds. My turn came in 1955 when, for the very first time, I laid eyes on the Chisos Mountains and the incredible landscapes that abound along the western edge of the Bofecillos Mountains and along the River Road between Lajitas and Presidio. Of course, in those days there was no paved road from Study Butte to Lajitas and on to Presidio.
> I spent two tours in Vietnam. Throughout the difficult times in Southeast Asia, images of Big Bend stayed alive for me—the sunset on the Chisos Mountains from the then ghost town of Terlingua, the full moon reflecting on the waters of the Rio Grande, the feel of a healthy catfish on the end of a line. When I was released from active duty on July 1, 1970, in California, I returned to the Big Bend and was firmly ensconced in camp upriver from Lajitas on the evening of the 2nd.

ACCORDING TO James Glendinning, a Scotsman living in Alpine and the author of *Mexico: Unofficial Border Crossings from the Big Bend*, Indians described the Chisos Mountains as "a heap of stones thrown down by the Great Spirits after they finished creating the Earth." The folks who gather on the porch of the Terlingua Store for sunset would not disagree.

FIELD NOTES—*Big Bend National Park. The western boundary of the park is seven miles east of the porch. Established in 1944, the 801,000-acre, 1,250-square-mile park is part desert, part sky island with a relict forest on top, and three breathtaking canyons, some with sheer walls rising as high as 1,500 feet along the 107 miles of the Rio Grande that form the park's southern boundary. There are more bird species (434) in Big Bend than in any other national park. Javelina, peregrine falcon, and black bear thrive, as do enough mountain lions to warrant posted warnings to visitors as to what to do in case of an encounter:* PICK UP SMALL CHILDREN.

"'Chasing around the desert' was a way of life for my uncle," says Kirby Warnock, the editor and publisher of the *Big Bend Quarterly* and nephew of the Big Bend's greatest naturalist, Dr. Barton H. Warnock:

> Raised in Fort Stockton, he attended Sul Ross State University on a football scholarship and set just about every rushing record for the Lobos on the field. In the classroom, he came under the tutelage of Dr. Omer Sperry, father of Texas gardening expert Neal Sperry.

CHISOS MOUNTAINS
Big Bend National Park

In 1938 he was chosen by Ross Maxwell to join a team of specialists cataloging all of the plants, animals, geology, and archaeological sites in a 350,000-acre tract of land that the federal government had just purchased that would later become Big Bend National Park. Operating from a government surplus army barracks in the Chisos Basin, Warnock went out into the rugged mountains and canyons to collect four samples of every plant that grew in the park. It was a voyage of exploration that extended into the Chinati, Glass, Davis, Barrilla, and Guadalupe mountains, as well as the Sierra del Carmen in Mexico, photographing and cataloging every known plant in the Trans-Pecos. He discovered dozens of unknown species, and twelve plants bear his name, including *Echinocactus warnockii,* or Warnock's cactus.

His biggest accomplishment was building the friendship and earning the respect of the ranchers who own nearly 90 percent of Texas's mountains. These ranchers granted him access to mountain peaks that were off-limits to the general public. Because of rising fears of the environmental movement and the federal government, there will probably never be another person who can do what he did.

He wrote and published three books considered essential for Big Bend aficionados: *Wildflowers of the Big Bend Country, Wildflowers of the Davis Mountains and Marathon Basin,* and *Wildflowers of the Guadalupe Mountains.* The science building at Sul Ross and the visitor center at Big Bend Ranch State Park are named in his honor. James Michener thought so much of Dr. Warnock that he used him as a source for his novel *Texas.* Former Texas governor Dolph Briscoe, the largest private landowner in the state, allowed him to build an arboretum and greenhouse on his Iron Mountain Ranch near Marathon to conserve native plants. Millionaire fund manager John Poindexter hired him to inventory all of the plants on Cibolo Creek Ranch after purchasing the historic property, and sought his advice on preserving the old *fortin* that Milton Faver built 150 years ago. Lady Bird Johnson regularly asked for his help on her campaign to save Texas wildflowers, and the late Supreme Court justice William O. Douglas corresponded with him about preserving Capote Falls, Texas's highest waterfall.

Botanists are usually portrayed as somewhat wimpy nerds, tooling around in a pith helmet, staring at plants through a huge magnifying glass. B. H. Warnock was a cowboy botanist, partial to khaki and a well-trimmed Stetson hat. He was fairly blunt with folks and didn't like for anyone or anything to slow him down. Before dedicating the visitor center at Big Bend Ranch, Parks and Wildlife director Andrew Sansom asked Dr. Warnock what he wanted out of the deal. "I just want to come and go as I please," he responded. "And I want you to keep people out of my way."

On a Tuesday morning in June of 1998, he was driving his car on Highway 67 between Alpine and Fort Stockton when he suffered a heart attack. His car went off the road and rolled to a stop in a pasture. They found him dead, with the motor still running. He died with his boots on, looking at the Davis Mountains. It was a pretty clean getaway for a man who lived a full life, doing what he wanted. I can't think of a better way to go.

BOFECILLOS MOUNTAINS
Big Bend Ranch State Park, Chorro Canyon

BIG BEND RANCH STATE PARK picks up where Big Bend National Park ends. The 280,281-acre spread, more than 400 square miles, all told, that encompasses the Bofecillos Mountains, an extinct volcano whose alluvial fans form a mountain plateau, opened to the public as a state park in 1991. More a ranch than a park, it is lower in elevation than the national park to the east but considerably wetter, with eighty-six year-round springs, four of the five highest waterfalls in the state, and fairy-tale microclimates choked with ferns and hardwoods hidden in well-shaded canyons. Its geological jewel, the Solitario, is an eroded lava dome nine miles in diameter that resembles a series of almost concentric rings when viewed from the air or seen on a map, and the seventh level of Hades when viewed from within.

"My favorite peak in Texas is Fresno Peak in the Solitario," says Jim Carrico, the former superintendent of Big Bend National Park and a partner in Desert Sports adventure outfitters in Terlingua, which hosts the Lajitas Chihuahuan Desert Challenge bike race. "It's the second highest in the state park at more than 5,120 feet (the highest, Oso, southwest of Sauceda, is less than 15 feet higher, at 5,135 feet). Fresno Peak is one of the more difficult places to get to in the Solitario, or in the state park. Despite the huge cairn on top (probably stacked there by Mexican goat herders when the Fowlkes brothers had their cattle operation here, or earlier), you get the sense that not many folks have recently made this hike. Perched on the south rim of the Solitario, you see views that are nearly indescribable. You look down on the Fresno Creek drainage and the flat-iron topography to the south; the whole Solitario formation lies behind. Of course, you can see the entire Chisos range to the east, and to the southwest lies the Sierra Rica in Mexico, another favorite. It's quite a spot. I'll have to admit I'm partial to places that require some effort to get to. Fresno Peak is a ball buster."

Once, on a hike from the Lower Shut-Up of the Solitario toward Lajitas, Carrico showed me bridge-trestle timbers and gravel remnants of the road that was built from Marfa to the river so General Pershing could chase after Pancho Villa.

For desert and mountain enthusiasts who think they've learned the lay of Big Bend National Park, the ranch is a whole 'nother world and way of looking at parks. Visitors either camp out, stay in the old ranch bunkhouse (men on one side; women on the other), or rent Sauceda, a.k.a. the Big House, the three-bedroom, two-bath headquarters of what was once the Fowlkes Cattle Company ranching empire. Activities include public Longhorn roundups (rent or BYOH—Bring Your Own Horse), camel excursions, and seminars on such subjects as photography, plant life, scorpions, and surviving in the desert.

David Alloway, the ranch's interpretive naturalist and author of *Desert Survival Skills*, teaches the desert survival seminar. He operates by a basic code essential to these parts: "Remember, *'Dum vita est, spes est.'* English translation: Where there is life there is hope. Texas translation: It ain't over 'til you're buzzard chow." I learned more about the desert by taking Alloway's three-day course at the ranch than in my entire life before—how to find water, read tracks, cook sotol and lechuguilla in a pit (tastes like a cross between an artichoke and a sweet potato), make a needle and thread and even rope from a lechuguilla, use the sap from a leatherstem, or *sangre de drago,* to numb a toothache. I learned everything but how to make a fire. The best I could muster was some smoke and what I'd swear was a faint ember before the blisters on my hands popped.

BOFECILLOS MOUNTAINS
Big Bend Ranch State Park, Rio Grande

PEOPLE WHO LIVE IN the Texas Mountains can discuss literature as eloquently as any intellectual in Austin, New York, or London, but no one talks books quite like Enrique Madrid, the town intellectual of Redford, whose own writings on the region—the "Exploring the West Texas Borderlands" chapter in the book *Hispanic Texas*, written with Curtis Tunnell of the Texas Historical Commission, and a paper, "Making and Taking Sotol in Chihuahua and Texas," from the Third Symposium on Resources of the Chihuahuan Desert—are authoritative works.

Unlike most intellectuals, Enrique backs up his words with deeds. To illustrate his points about living off the desert, he asks his wife, Ruby, to bring me honey, a glass, a bottle of sotol (and it's not even noon), tortillas, quince fruit paste, even a smooth, egg-shaped river stone—the last item to underscore why Chicanos, *mexicanos*, and *indios* don't need milk for calcium. The stone is limestone and when it's heated to the boiling point, the lime leaches out and can be added to corn to make the essential ingredients of tortillas, a staple of the native diet.

As for the clear sotol liquor derived from the desert plant of the same name, he says: "During Prohibition, this kept Texas alive, or in a stupor. Try some." I do and swallow hard. "It's like kissing a scorpion," he smiles. No kidding. The honey is another kind of medicine. "It's from mesquite, acacia, and catclaw. It's very robust. It's said to be good for allergies." And much, much smoother than sotol.

For the next two hours, Madrid feeds me *machaca* (dried beef), quince fruit leather, *pinole* (whole-wheat grain), *nopalitos* (prickly pear cactus pads), *asadero* cheese made with

CHISOS MOUNTAINS
Big Bend National Park

BOFECILLOS MOUNTAINS AND SIERRA RICA
Big Bend Ranch State Park

the berries of silverleaf nightshade, and candies made of pumpkin, sweet potatoes, and barrel cactus, throwing books on my lap as he does so. "These are the desert plants we still eat. We've been eating them for 12,000 years and we still love it."

Madrid's mother, Lucía Madrid, was the community librarian of Redford, celebrated for assembling one of the largest collections of books in the Big Bend. His great-grandparents moved to Redford from Chihuahua 155 years ago. Literature has always been part of family life.

Redford is old culture and old blood, he says. "This valley is formed by the two rivers that join here at La Junta. It's been cultivated for a long time. Two Puebloan groups, the Jornada and the Mogollon, settled here about 1200 A.D. They did a DNA study of the people of Ojinaga and Juárez, across from El Paso. Scientists found that 87 percent of the people here and there still belong to one of the four major native groups. [In Ojinaga, it's actually 91 percent of the population, according to a 1997 study.] The culture, the folklore to a large extent, the religion are all still here. People here have nicknames—that's from Indian tradition. You never call a person by their formal name, publicly. My nickname is Chapo—Shorty. We're still Indians."

He hands me a bound volume, *Alvar Nuñez Cabeza de Vaca.* "He was the first European that interacted with the Indians. Previous explorers regarded Indians as something less than human, someone to be subjugated. Cabeza de Vaca came to see them as human beings. He lived with Indians long enough to understand they were like him. He was the first modern man who created the consciousness of a new kind of human being."

Five visitors have shuffled in since Madrid started his discourse—a disaffected couple from Weatherford (he's a native Texan, she's from England) and their son, looking to settle in a trailer on the desert, and two older Anglo gentlemen come to pay respects to Enrique's mother, the librarian. All listen intently.

"We have the same thing today: two powerful cultures, Mexican and American, divided by language, values, economies. But here on the border, every day, we're creating a new kind of human being. We're Cabeza de Vaca's children. Those of us who live on the border, we're creating a new language—Tex-Mex, Spanglish, Gringlish—without having both, you won't understand what's being said. We're creating a new cuisine with jalapeño pizza and roast beef burritos. You have two powerful cultures living on the border, and if we don't kill each other, we will create this new culture."

He knows only too well about the killing. On May 20, 1997, Esequiel Hernández Jr., an eighteen-year-old herding goats with a rifle on his family's land near the river, was mistaken for a drug smuggler and shot and killed by one of four Marines who'd been called in to patrol United States soil as part of the government's war on drugs.

Madrid shows me a black-and-white photograph of a woman reading to two children. The woman is his mother. One of the children is a much younger Esequiel. "She received two presidential medals of honor, recognized by President George Bush, for her teaching and her library." He fetches the documentation. "The real tragedy is this: George Bush started the program that created that task force at Fort Bliss with Colin Powell the liaison between the military and civil law enforcement agencies in 1989. He created the program that brought the Marines to Redford. Joint Task Force Six grew out of Bush's National Drug Control Strategy. This is what happened, as a result of his actions."

BOFECILLOS MOUNTAINS
Big Bend Ranch State Park, Las Cuevas

Madrid pulls out an article from a 1991 edition of the *Denver Post* with the headline LIBRARY AN OASIS IN DRUG CAPITAL. A customs agent is quoted as saying Redford is the drug-smuggling capital of the Southwest and that three-quarters of the town's population are allegedly traffickers in the business of transporting illicit marijuana, cocaine, and heroin across the river and on to faraway cities on the American side. "That means all but twenty-five of us are *narcotraficantes*. It's rhetoric."

A copy of *Ancient Texas* follows. He finds a passage about the pictographs in hundreds of caves around the Pecos River and Lower Pecos Indians ingesting botanic hallucinogens during shamanistic religious ceremonies over 10,000 years or so. "The war on drugs on the border is a continuation of this religious-cultural war on Native Americans that the Spanish tried to suppress, the padres tried to suppress, and the drug czar tries to suppress."

Another report is thrown on my lap. The population on both sides of the border is growing faster than the population of either country as a whole, doubling every twenty years. Presidio, which grew from 3,075 to 5,400 residents between 1991 and 2000, is on the verge of eclipsing Alpine as the biggest town in the Texas Mountains outside of El Paso.

"The United States of North America. This is the legacy of Cabeza de Vaca. My uncles and aunts and grandfather, our wives lived across the river for generations. The American border is only 150 years old. We cannot survive divided.

"The week Esequiel was killed, the House of Representatives of the United States Congress passed an amendment to add 10,000 troops, five armed Marines every mile [along the Rio Grande]. It's not a military problem. It's a medical and cultural problem. They're not going to solve the problem with the military. Because of the physical proximity of these nations, the unification will happen here first, economically, socially. You already have capital crossing borders. War is obsolete."

He produces a page full of statistics. "Twenty-four percent of the population in United States border counties in 1998 lived in poverty, compared to 14 percent nationally. In Texas, the border population living in poverty is 35 percent. It's 48 percent in Presidio County. All this after 150 years of American rule of this territory. So you don't need a war on drugs. You need a war on poverty, like LBJ did in Appalachia."

Lucía Madrid's store closed in 1989. The library closed in 1998. By then Redford's school, isolated as it is, was wired to the Internet.

SIMONE SWAN'S LIFE changed forever the first time she laid eyes on Fort Leaton, an adobe compound overlooking the Rio Grande thirteen miles west of Redford and two miles east of Presidio that was neither a fort nor Ben Leaton's property. She vacated her apartment at Eighty-ninth and Fifth in New York City and left her career in fine arts administration (she's the founding director of the Menil Foundation) and put down roots on the Terneros lowlands by the Rio Grande. She was determined to build affordable adobe housing for those in need, like her Egyptian mentor, Hassan Fathy, one of the world's authorities on earth architecture, had done. But salvation through mud was not to be.

"I did quite a bit of outreach," she told me. "After a year, an associate told me that some people tend to find adobe lamentable. *Lamentable*. Very few want to owner-build, or build cooperatively. Most people want to move into manufactured trailers and not face the fact they have $500 payments forever at 19 percent interest for a dwelling that loses value.

CHISOS MOUNTAINS
Big Bend National Park, South Rim

I will get the government to finance my housing as soon as the engineers at Texas A&M provide certification for the roofs, even though there are vaulted ceilings like these still standing in Egypt 4,000 years after they were built."

Swan is undeterred, because adobe is in her blood and Presidio is ideal for adobe. So she's building homes, one at a time, mostly for affluent out-of-town clients wanting a home really away from home. It's like her project director, Jesusita Jimenez, says: "*Estamos hermanas de adobe*—we're sisters of adobe."

The Texas Mountains have a lot to do with it. "The mountains here, I don't think, are overwhelming, in the sense that the mountains in Colorado are," Swan says. "There's something here, though, that's so calm. They inspire respect. I've lived on three continents. I've seen the Amalfi Drive plunge into the Mediterranean. I've seen the mountains of the moon in the Kivu region of the Congo. To my mind, nothing equals the River Drive [El Camino del Río, the fifty miles of Farm Road 170 between Presidio and Lajitas] in variety, in color, and, of course, isolation."

CHISOS MOUNTAINS
Big Bend National Park

FIELD NOTES—*El Camino del Río. The road is best experienced by going east from Presidio to Lajitas. It begins unremarkably along the river flats past Fort Leaton, each turn unveiling a vista a little more impressive until Redford fades in the rearview mirror. Then, while the river meanders tranquilly, the two-lane blacktop begins to twist, turn, climb, and drop, snaking through tight canyons framed by peaks as jagged as glass shards, into a landmass almost devoid of human population. It's a busy day when more than ten vehicles pass in the other direction. Evidence of upheavals from a time when hell on earth really existed is everywhere, manifested in shapes and forms not of this world. Some points of the passage are so narrow that it becomes clear the Bofecillos on the American side and the Sierra Rica on the Mexican side are one and the same, their names a matter of geographic convenience.*

The climax is Big Hill, or, as the yellow diamond sign by the road simply states: HILL—*a benign description for a 15 percent gradient. Pull off at the wide area on the south side of the road before reaching the crest, walk over to the railing, look back west over Colorado Canyon, and have a spiritual experience. Halfway up a steep wall on the Mexican side of the river, a mile or so upriver, a significant chunk of mountain has fallen away, as up-front and personal as erosion can be.*

BOFECILLOS MOUNTAINS
Big Bend Ranch State Park, Ojito Adentro
(Spring)

Radio Ranchito, 1260-AM, the radio station from Ojinaga, is the only signal you can pick up along most of the route, at least until you get to the fifteen-watt KYOTE, Terlingua's pirate radio station. Radio Ranchito plays a lot of local *banda, norteño,* and *conjunto* music that is indigenous to Mexico, much of it topical material, including paeans to *narcotraficantes,* people not uncommon to this region.

In September 2000 three drug traffickers from Ojinaga known as *los tres de la sierra,* the three of the mountain, were apprehended in Sydney, Australia and Hawaii after being seen on worldwide television unfurling a VIVA OJINAGA banner and wearing Mexican sombreros. They were small potatoes compared to Pablo Acosta, the drug lord of Ojinaga who in 1987 was gunned down in Santa Elena, across the river from Big Bend National Park, by Mexican troops flown in from the United States in helicopters provided by the United States, and whose exploits were celebrated in *corridos* on the border when he was still alive; or Rick Thompson, the sheriff of Presidio County, who in 1992 was caught on the county fairgrounds in Marfa pulling a horse trailer containing more than a ton of cocaine.

On the River Road, all of that is another world away. The ear hears an announcement on Radio Ranchito for a weekend baseball tournament pitting teams from Lajitas, San Carlos, Ojinaga, and Presidio against each other. The eye is drawn to two boys on horses who suddenly appear by the roadside. For the past hour there have been no dwellings, no power lines, no radio towers, only a collection of adobe ruins on a river bluff, the leftover movie set from the film *Contrabandista.*

Lajitas, the "Ultimate Hideout," with a golf course, swimming pool, desert museum, airstrip, horse stables, condos, motel rooms, and a genuine fake Western town boardwalk, is the first sign of civilization.

The resort was built during the 1970s by Houston developer Walter Mischer, who declared it "the Palm Springs of Texas." But Lajitas never took off, and in 2000 Mischer auctioned off his holdings. The winning bidder was an Austin entrepreneur named Steve Smith, who made his fortune in a telecommunications company; he paid $4.2 million for the town.

Lajitas was already something of a hub before it became a resort. The rock bed in the river has been the most dependable crossing on the Rio Grande between Del Rio and El Paso. The general store near the crossing, where tourists proffer beer to Clay Henry Jr., the resident goat, opened for business in 1899.

Many visitors continue to cross here, paying a man wearing a Border Patrol gimme cap two dollars to row them over to Paso Lajitas so they can eat lunch or dinner at one of two restaurants or take a day trip to San Carlos, a spring-fed mountain town twelve miles into the interior.

Sometime in the mid-1990s, I'd read a front-page story in the *Dallas Morning News* stating that federal officials wanted to close this and other "unofficial" crossings along the Texas-Mexico border. That same day, I asked the gruff old man tending the register at the Lajitas store what would happen if the crossing was closed. He bellowed loudly, "Aw, the boat man would move his boat a couple hundred yards up the river and keep doing what he's been doing. You can't close this down. People have been crossing here since before there was a United States."

KEN BARNES IS bursting with pride over his just-opened Badlands Fossils, a room full of big, big bones and other fossils that the self-taught paleontologist has dug up on private lands in the Big Bend. There is a fine impression of a Sabal palm, fossils of a 35-foot duck-billed dinosaur that school kids from Abilene are helping to dig up, a notation that "It was a mosasaur eat mosasaur world, 80+mya," meaning "80 million years or so ago," and a skull of a tylosaur marine lizard from 85 million years ago, its incisors still sharp.

I ask Barnes about the theory that dinosaurs were wiped out from the effects of a large meteor falling into the Gulf of Mexico. "The meteor did hit, yes," he tells me. "But dinosaurs were already going out on their own. Water was drying up. Flowering plants were appearing, but dinosaurs weren't able to exploit them." He shrugs. "But I'm an amateur. What do I know?"

MARFA is different. TIE YOUR HORSE AND COME ON IN, reads the sign in front of Carmen's Mexican cafe on U.S. Highway 90. MARFA IS WHAT THE WEST WAS, says the small billboard in front of the local chamber of commerce, three blocks down. ENJOY MARFA, ABOUT THE SAME ALTITUDE AS DENVER, is the message written on the window of the lobby of the Holiday/Capri Motel.

The town is an island in a sea of tall grasses, ranching country that has created cattle kingdoms that have dominated the social and political ways of the region for the past century and inspired the epic book and movie *Giant*.

The town's got style, too, from the domed courthouse three blocks from Highway 90, to the adobe and stucco architecture of half the storefronts, and the particularly splendid design of the Hotel Paisano imagined by Southwestern architect Henry Trost, to (more recently) the creations of sculptor Donald Judd, who bought up property when the town

64

was dying and reinvented old Fort Russell as a permanent exhibition space for his own works and those of his friends, overseen by the Chinati Foundation.

Stand under the Claes Oldenburg giant horseshoe sculpture *Monument to the Last Horse* and look east, framing Cathedral Mountain inside the horseshoe, and you'll understand. Just don't let it go to your head.

"We're not someone's Kodak moment," Robert Halpern insists. Robert is the editor and publisher of the *Big Bend Sentinel.* His wife, Rosario Salgado Halpern, is the chief financial officer and sometimes reporter. They also oversee another newspaper, the *International,* in Presidio. Theirs may be the only small-town newspaper office in Texas with abstract art hanging on the walls. They live in a part of town called Sal Si Puedes, traditionally the poor Mexican side of Marfa, separated from the rest of town by a creek that sometimes floods (thus its name—Leave If You Can). Their home, designed by an architect from Los Angeles and built by a crew from Ojinaga, looks like an art museum, with huge windows that let the sharp light in.

WWDJD?

—"WHAT WOULD DONALD JUDD DO?" BUMPER STICKER SOLD DURING
CHINATI/JUDD FOUNDATIONS OPEN HOUSE, REFLECTING A
YET-TO-BE-SETTLED ESTATE SEVEN YEARS AFTER JUDD'S DEATH

CHINATI MOUNTAINS
Prickly pear cactus

DONALD JUDD IS PARTLY to blame. Despite his international renown as a sculptor of big, abstract art, Judd hated museums and galleries. In the 1960s, he rebelled, purchased an old warehouse in the SoHo district of New York, and invited his friends to put their works on permanent display there. When he ran out of room, he started looking elsewhere. Marfa didn't just have space, it had a closed army camp waiting for a new tenant. Most of the buildings that had once housed commercial businesses were vacant. Judd bought them up and started filling them with art like John Chamberlain's twisted metal sculptures, which resemble nothing so much as wrecked cars. One of the barracks of the old military camp was re-created as a freshly abandoned Russian schoolhouse by Russian environmental artist Ilya Kabokov. Judd's larger works occupy the hangars at the fort. Dan Flavin utilized several barracks for a permanent fluorescent light installation that has drawn international praise from critics.

The Halperns put out the best newspaper in the Trans-Pecos, weekly or otherwise (although the gossipy *Terlingua Moon* posted on bulletin boards—official slogan: COLLECTING THE FACTS, THEN DISTORTING THEM AS WE PLEASE—and the feisty online muckraker *Nimby News* are close runners-up). It's got a lot to do with what they have had to work with. Consider these events, all of which occurred within a recent two-month span: the former sector chief of the Border Patrol elected as county judge; fifty national committee members of the Whitney Museum of American Art flying in to Marfa on six corporate jets to see the Chinati art collection; the murder, attempted murder, and suicide at the hydroponic tomato farm of three *mexicanos* involved in a love triangle; and the announcement that the town of Presidio on the border effectively doubled its population in ten years.

It's got a lot to do with Robert growing up in Alpine and Rosario growing up in Presidio, too. They know how things are different in Far West Texas. Like enchiladas. "Red enchiladas are flat, not rolled, with an egg on top," Robert says. "That's real Texan, but only in Far West Texas. You can keep your motor running. Out here, you don't have to lock your car."

You do have to know your realism from your impressionism, though. "We're becoming the darling of the art world," Robert says. "We're the hip place to be. A lot of it is the [Dan] Flavin installation. That got all this publicity in *Vanity Fair* and the *New Yorker*. [The author] David Foster Wallace was here last summer. Denise Chavez [the New Mexico poet and writer] is here now. The Judd family and the Chinati Foundation are settling Donald Judd's estate. The Lannan Foundation houses a writer-in-residence. This is good for the economy. This is good for Marfa."

And ranching? Isn't this *Giant* country?

"I don't think ranching is going to die, but there's no more King Cotton. There's no more King Oil. There's no more King Cattle. It's another business. What's interesting is you've got the Tiguas [one of two recognized Indian tribes of Texas] coming in [and buying the Chillicote Ranch in the Sierra Vieja], you've got the Nature Conservancy [creating conservation easements on private lands in the Davis and Chinati mountains]. All these newcomers. No one has the lock and key. We have to make the best of it."

Rosario isn't complaining. "We came here twelve years ago and the town was dying. Since then, the newspaper has gone from eight-page editions to sixteen-page editions. The Chinati Foundation brings the world to Marfa. We just sit here and everyone comes by. We

CHINATI MOUNTAINS
Pinto Canyon

67

have friends in Switzerland and Sweden. We meet the artists and collect their works. Our daughter is studying art history at Brown University. Living here influenced her. At a real young age, she started volunteering at the foundation, giving tours."

"We choose to live here because we don't like traffic, but it doesn't mean we don't know what's going on in the world," Robert says. "Even the old ranches have Web sites, or offer accommodations-the Maravillas Guest Ranch, J. P. Bryan [the entrepreneur who bought up the Gage Hotel in Marathon and other buildings and land and transformed the dying railroad town into a hub of tourism as the Gateway to Big Bend National Park], Al Micalleff [owner of the CF Ranch, one of the region's biggest, and the Reata restaurants in Alpine, Fort Worth, and Beverly Hills]."

This is just like Greenwich Village in the 1960s.
—OVERHEARD AT A MARFA ART OPENING, OCTOBER 2000

THE NEW SOCIAL CENTER of Marfa is the bookstore–coffee shop two blocks from the courthouse. It draws perhaps the most eclectic crowd in the Trans-Pecos, everybody from People in Black from New York and Europe to hardscrabble cowboys craving a double latte. But around the corner and past all the talk of galleries and light and museums and what Don would have done, time has stood still. Two boys meander along the road, practicing their skills with a lasso out of boredom, jumping in and out of the rope circle they are twirling.

FIELD NOTES—*Chinati Mountains, Pinto Canyon Road. It takes the permission of four different property owners and a woman at the office of the Donald Judd estate in order to see Vizcaino Canyon, where the Chinatis meet the Sierra Vieja and Donald Judd is buried. We also have to buy a lock and borrow bolt cutters. "It's to cut the lock this asshole neighbor keeps putting on a gate where we have an easement to get to our property," explains Craig Rember, an employee of the estate.*

Boyd Elder, a visual artist from Valentine whose buffalo skulls decorate the covers of several albums of the music group the Eagles—including their Greatest Hits package, the best-selling album in the history of recorded music—tells Laurence and me that we have to see it. It's a spiritual place. The ranch is fifty miles from Marfa, but less than half of those miles are on pavement. The trail across the remaining miles, dropping through Pinto Canyon onto the Rio Grande floodplain, is loose gravel at best, requiring considerable caution and four-wheel drive, bolt cutters notwithstanding. We descend into the canyon in midafternoon, just in time to witness a magnificent shower throwing a veil over the Chinatis and obscuring the top of Chinati Peak. It is such a rare event that we don't mind getting soaked just to watch it rain.

When we finally get within four miles of the river, past the turnoff to Chinati Hot Springs, the road to Vizcaino turns even rougher and harder to follow. It finally gives out, disappearing in an impassable mound of gravel filling a low-water crossing. We turn around and head back toward Marfa. A Border Patrol vehicle drives out to greet us south of Marfa, passing us, then turning around and following us into town. We've obviously triggered sensors on the road. It's the first vehicle we've seen since leaving Marfa five hours earlier.

CHINATI MOUNTAINS
Cibolo Creek Ranch, restored fort

CHINATI MOUNTAINS
Cibolo Creek Ranch
Restored fort, courtyard doorway

The lodging of choice for high rollers in the Trans-Pecos is Cibolo Creek Ranch, thirty miles south of Marfa. The ranch is really an adobe fort, El Fortin del Cibolo, with watch-towers and fortified walls three feet thick. It was built by Milton Faver, the first Anglo rancher in the area, in the 1850s, along with two other fortresses, La Cienega and La Morita, constructed around three significant springs on the eastern flank of the Chinatis to keep out Indians and bandits traveling the Comanche Trail. At its peak, Faver ran as many as 200,000 head of Longhorns on his ranch before his death in 1889.

One hundred one years later, the 25,000-acre desert ranch was bought by Southwest-ern Holdings, a Houston corporation headed by John Poindexter, who has overseen the reconstruction and transformation of all three forts into a luxury resort with sixteen rooms, a wine cellar, and a landing strip long enough for jets. The rock singer Mick Jagger and his family spent several weeks at La Cienega and offered to buy the place from Poindexter, and a member of the country music group the Dixie Chicks held her wedding on the grounds.

I like West Texas. Where else can you get up in the mornin' and see clear from yesterday to tomorrow?

—U.S. DISTRICT JUDGE LUCIUS BUNTON (1924–2001),
THE REAL LAW WEST OF THE PECOS, WHO WAS RAISED ON A RANCH NEAR SHAFTER

69

THE HISTORY OF the ghost mining town of Shafter, halfway between Marfa and Presidio on U.S. Highway 67 and no more than ten miles down Cibolo Creek from the ranch resort, can be discovered by unlatching a series of wooden cabinets at the Brooks Cemetery across Cibolo Creek from the old town. Each cabinet has pictures and text detailing the storied past of what was once the biggest silver mine in the United States and the town that grew around it.

At the beginning of the twentieth century, 2,000 people lived in Shafter, 225 men worked at the mine, and 75 worked at the mill. Two schools operated, one for Anglos, one for Mexicans. The community had a boardinghouse, a general store, a meat market, a hospital, a men's clubhouse with pool tables, a baseball field, a tennis court that doubled as a dance floor, and a golf course. Amusements included baseball, dancing, hiking, riding burros, drinking sotol, making music, singing in the church choir, and whatever pleasures could be obtained from bootleggers. Poetry readings were said to be a popular pastime. To keep the town going, four thousand cords of wood a year were logged out of the Chinati Mountains until there were no trees of significant size left, and later, along the Rio Grande.

At the beginning of the twenty-first century, there are forty residents in Shafter. The ghost town is slowly being repopulated after being abandoned when the mine closed in 1942. The church remains the center of town activities. The post office has been closed.

Bob Tucker is spearheading the restoration of some of the town's more historic structures, including the schoolhouse, where he resides. He'd like to get the displays at the

Brooks Cemetery moved next to his residence, since the school is right on the highway. He says not to tell anyone, but he's hearing that the mine will reopen.

AL REAL HAS HEARD the same. Al runs the Mesquite Ranch, about fifteen miles over the Chi-natis from Tucker, and he's been chasing off prospectors looking for minerals there. They ought to know better than trifle with Al, a no-bull cowboy who knows the foothills of the Chinatis and the river country like few others and walks in his sleep. Besides, if the rogues did find ore or even a vein, the state would claim it, since 33,000 acres of the ranch are owned by Texas Parks and Wildlife and are being held in reserve as a future recreational destination.

For now, it's still pretty much a ranch, and if there're strangers on the land, they're more likely to be wets, or wetbacks, as Mexican nationals crossing into the United States without legal papers are called, than prospectors, since the headquarters is ten miles from the river. "Two wets passed through the other day, tired and thirsty," Real says. "They'd been taken into the Chinatis by a coyote, who left them, telling them he'd be back with water. He never returned; 'course he'd already been paid. I told them I'd have to call the Border Patrol, but they didn't mind. They were too tired. It was the humane thing to do. If they'd died of dehydration on the ranch, I'd have a hard time forgiving myself."

Luis Armendariz, the superintendent of Big Bend Ranch State Park and the steward of record for what is officially known as the Chinati Mountains State Natural Area, has been on the Mesquite Ranch land only five times since Heiner and Philippa Friedrich sold their ranch to the Richard King Mellon Foundation, which donated the land to the state in 1996. The Friedrichs held on to 3,000 acres for themselves and created an endowment to the county to allay the loss of property taxes, a frequently voiced reason that property owners give for their opposition to the creation of parklands.

In the 1970s, Al Real oversaw construction of four rock cabins and several shade shelters by Mexican masons and rock artisans at scenic points on higher plateaus above the river valley. In winter, the Friedrichs and some of their friends and associates, including several Middle Eastern princes, princesses, and sheikhs, fly into Presidio in private jets to observe Ramadan holy days of their chosen Islamic faith. Copies of the Koran are in each cabin.

This place was made for meditation, I think.

FIELD NOTES—*Chinati Mountains State Natural Area. Climb a small peak on the edge of San Antonio Canyon, like Laurence does diligently before sunrise and before sunset every day, and the process of erosion becomes easier to understand. Cracks and fissures sharpen into focus. Millions of years of drainage wearing and tearing is easy to see in each smoothed hill and every broad pile of alluvial fill, some of it miles wide. The lechuguilla, spiky yucca, and leatherstem at my feet serve notice: I can never climb high enough in the Chinatis to escape the desert.*

On a gray day when scudding clouds are shredded by the crest of Chinati Peak and winds blur the lines in the distance, a drought persisting, a covey of ten, twenty, no, thirty bobwhite quail march past me single file to a watering trough, seeking a morning drink as a reminder that, even here, life persists.

CUESTA DEL BURRO

Luis Armendariz comes from one of the oldest families in Presidio. While driving Laurence and me to the ranch, he tells me he's been getting some mighty tempting offers to lease the rights to take water out of the Rio Grande to irrigate his family farm in the river plain. A group from Laredo wants it. He just may do it.

The farms that once cultivated cotton, onions, cantaloupes, and vegetables by the river are going fallow. "There used to be forty farmers working the plain," Armendariz says. Othal Brand, an agribusiness operator from South Texas, came in and bought out many of the farmers in the 1950s and 1960s, before going broke himself in the 1990s, he tells me. Luis, his brothers Frank and Carlos, and Bill Bishop are the last farmers left. Luis grows onions mainly, but it's a losing proposition. His buyer, located in Michigan, purchases produce from all over the world, and in that world market, where many countries' labor costs are considerably lower than those of the Texas-Mexico border, it's hard to compete.

72

Much hope has been placed in the *maquiladora* system of foreign corporations, including many American businesses, setting up assembly plants in Mexico to exploit cheap labor. But the biggest plant in Ojinaga, across from Presidio, where Chinese bicycles were put together, closed in early 2000, putting more than eight hundred workers out of jobs.

Luis thinks tourism is a better bet. "The infrastructure is here. Nature is all around us. You don't have to spend much economically to attract visitors."

The Rio Grande is not the provider it once was. The troubles began in the 1940s when Elephant Butte dam was constructed upriver in southern New Mexico, effectively shutting off the normal flow of water out of the Rockies. In 1971 the International Boundary and Water Commission rechanneled the river at La Junta above Presidio and Ojinaga, where the Río Conchos joins the Rio Grande, and the cyclical flooding of the plain, which replenished the soil with nutrients, ceased.

The river, called the Río Bravo, Brave River, on the other side, is now described by many as the Río Puerco, Pig River, because it's so polluted and laden with salts, says Al Real. His Mexican ranch hands won't even eat fish caught in the river anymore.

SIERRA VIEJA
Coal Mine Ranch

FIELD NOTES—*Sierra Vieja, as seen from U.S. Highway 90. First impression: a low, tilting, dry range gradually rising up 1,000 feet or so above the llano, where the deer and the antelope really do play, with four prominent flanks whose tops appear to have been evenly sheared by God the Barber, stretching almost all the way east of Valentine to Van Horn. When backlit by a soft pink-orange glow, the last remnants of a setting sun tinting the wisps of high clouds riding the jet stream from the west, they are sublime.*

Highway 90 is straight as an arrow, the contour of the earth it cuts through interrupted only by the occasional yucca spiking up off the desert floor, an endless line of telephone poles, and a locomotive pulling a long train of freight. A pair of hawks soar on invisible currents toward the sierra while tumbleweeds tumble across the road.

Man-made objects are so few and far between, they're hard to miss: a trailer protected by a lone mercury vapor light on the plain; the weird incongruity of a big fat blimp the size of a 747—a radar aerostat intended to catch drug smugglers—floating above the basin, tethered to the ground. Half of the town of Valentine seems gone with the old railroad economy that once made it prosper.

A rock shop on the highway advertises its goods as "wholesale." Nobody stirs inside. The ruins of a fifties-vintage roadside attraction, all angles and lines, are a mystery. Was this a motel, a cafe, a gas station, or a tourist trap of another kind?

Perfect rows of pecan trees standing at military attention showcase the triumph of irrigated agriculture on the desert. Remnants of sluice gates and plow marks in the sand speak volumes of its foibles.

Clay E. Miller, the elder of one of the ranching dynasties in the Sierra Vieja, keeps a record of moisture that his father started in 1936. "If you could determine a pattern from this, I'd surely appreciate it," he deadpans when he hands it to me.

Certain numbers jump off the handwritten pages: 6.07 inches in 1956, driest on record, followed by 6.99 in 1957, the peak of the most severe drought on record in Texas. A meager

73

6.47 in 1989, a semitropical 31.12 inches the next year. Less than 10 inches in 1998 and only 13.21 in 1999, .27 of an inch the first five months of 2000 and then—*whomp!*—5.10 inches in June 2000. Nothing again for the next three months, then it pours.

The wettest months are July, August, and September, when the monsoonal flow of warm, unstable air blows up from the Pacific coast of Mexico over the Sierra Madre. Heaviest rains come from the southeast and the Gulf of Mexico. "The best pattern for us is for a hurricane to hit south of the mouth of the Rio Grande, or up to fifty miles north," Miller allows. "If that happens, we'll get an inch or two here." The fifty-year average annual rainfall from 1938 to 1986 is 13.33 inches.

It's never enough. "Everyone's subject to economic hard times when you're in a drouth"—as Miller pronounces it. "You don't know how long it's going to last. Last year we got 13.24. That's average. But two or three miles down the road, they didn't get two inches." June rains created a playa lake in the flats that hadn't appeared in eight years.

Frost is common from November to April. "We get a blue norther on occasion, but there's probably more that just miss us and slide down to the east," he says. "We had eighteen inches of snowfall in the winter of 1982–83. It's been below zero three or four times in my lifetime, but the last three, four years, we've had an exceedingly mild winter. Our usual winter lows are somewhere between ten degrees and zero."

Summers are the mildest in Texas, cool and dry at night no matter how hot it gets during the day, cool enough to run the British breeds. "That's one reason Brahma are so popular south of here, where it's more humid. For range, it's fine cow country."

At the end of each seasonal entry is a small space for comments on spring conditions, usually a simple "fair," "good," "second best," "loco," and the occasional "disaster." "Loco" refers to an abundance of locoweed on the range, which spells economic ruin. "The cows are like people on dope," Miller says. "They fail to eat, lose weight, all they want to do is eat locoweed. When they get addicted, they're far less valuable."

So long as you factor in marginal profits and the cyclical market, the cattle business is all about the reproductive cycle of cows. "Prices go down and a lot of people reduce their stock. Folks hold their females back for reproductive purposes, and prices go up. Early in the century, the average slaughter animal was four or five years old. Now, it's unusual for a cow to be more than two years old. So the cycles become more compressed."

Over a bluff behind the main house is a spring and the ruins of a military installation known as Camp Holland. The army was called in following a raid by Mexican *banditos* on the store of the Brite Ranch on Christmas Day of 1917, not far from the Miller Ranch. Construction began in 1918, primarily to protect pack trains from Valentine going through Viejo Pass and over the rimrock to supply troops patrolling the Rio Grande during the period of border troubles sparked by the Mexican Revolution.

"It wasn't an invasion concern so much as banditry," Miller explains. Facilities on the permanent grounds included housing for four hundred troops, officers' houses, and a bakery. Three years later, the border quieted down, the military left, and the camp was auctioned off, though the stone and wood buildings remain.

The spring marks the site where four Pueblo scouts working with the Twenty-fourth United States Infantry were killed by Mescalero Apaches after the cavalry abandoned them

SIERRA VIEJA
Coal Mine Ranch, pond from geothermal well

SIERRA VIEJA
ZH Canyon

SIERRA VIEJA
Gettysburg Peak, Coal Mine Ranch

in 1880. It was the last Apache battle in Presidio County. One of the four scouts, Simon Olgun, is revered as the *cacique*, or spiritual leader, of the present-day Tigua tribe.

The Tigua are descendants of peaceful farmers from the Ysleta Pueblo, below El Paso on the Rio Grande, who were outnumbered and eventually overwhelmed to the point of vanishing, only to be belatedly recognized as a tribe by the U.S. government in the 1980s. Now they are thriving, thanks to a gambling casino established on their El Paso "reservation." Profits allowed the tribe to purchase the 70,000-acre Chillicote Ranch, next to Miller's ranch, as a tribal retreat, creating the largest private game preserve in Texas.

There's been talk of a high-dollar resort, another gambling casino, or a water mining operation like El Paso is setting up on the Antelope Valley Ranch nearby. Tribal sources insist that Chillicote was purchased only as a refuge and because it is near the battle site on the Miller Ranch, which, as they see it, is sacred ground.

ON THE BACK SIDE of the Sierra Vieja, a world away from the lush pastures of the Miller Ranch and twenty-six miles from the end of the pavement on Chispa Road, a route not

76

found on highway maps, is the Coal Mine Ranch, featuring its own tunnel, twenty feet high and fifty yards deep, blasted from solid rock. Which leads one to wonder about the sanity of the promoters who in 1893 decided to build a spur from the railroad near Valentine to a coal mine on the ranch, finishing two years later. The only problem, Fred Nelan says, is "there's no evidence that coal was ever hauled out."

Nelan is part of a group of businessmen who've owned the ranch for more than twenty years, as an investment and as a playground. The 27,500-acre spread is officially a cattle operation managed by Elvis Tarango, who is also the *alcalde*, or mayor, of the Los Fresnos *ejido* (farm collective) across the Rio Grande. But to Nelan especially, ranching also describes the infrequent weekend soirees in the bunkhouse of the headquarters with friends and family, a ritual common on many of the larger ranches in Texas.

There's plenty to do: visit a bat cave, peer into a mine shaft four hundred feet deep; pore over the crumbling stone ruins of a small community that housed railroad workers and search for the graves of Chinese laborers (which are allegedly nearby); examine the hoist, draw wheels, coke ovens, and other detritus from futile attempts to establish mining operations; or scour a low slope below the sandstone bluffs for fossils of clams, turtle shells, coral, and snails—eighty-five-million-year-old souvenirs from an ancient mudhole in a river delta said to be six hundred miles wide, bigger than the Amazon River. Mostly, though, this kind of ranching is about solitude, introspection, and long talks around the campfire.

For Nelan, an accountant who sets up factories in Mexico for international corporations, it's also an excuse to leave the numbers behind and get down and dirty, whether it's helping Elvis Tarango build or fix roads, welding irrigation pipes, mending fences, hunting game, or working on the ranch trucks. "You have to be half engineer to ranch out here."

The railroad builders certainly were. "It could have been a scam between the railroad, the construction crew, and the mining company," he speculates. His daughter did extensive research on the subject. "At the time, railroad bonds were a big deal for investors. And my daughter has found there were investors in Pittsburgh, in El Paso, in Marfa."

A century later, the search for a fuel that burns hot, given the region's history of vulcanism, continues.

"Just last month, geologists from Cementos de Chihuahua [the Mexican state across the river] came in here and drilled six bore holes to test for coal," Nelan says. "They must have spent sixty thousand dollars building roads, boring holes. They tested and tested, knowing from the exposed veins that the coal was very, very good—almost anthracite. But no dice."

"So one hundred years later, they reached the same conclusion as the railroad," laughs Joe Christie, the former state senator who is one of Nelan's partners in the ranch. "There isn't enough coal to mine."

There's evidence that Spanish conquistadors were the first to covet the ranch's coal. A brick smelter found close to an exposed vein, Nelan says, is of Spanish, not Anglo, origin. "Geologists and archaeologists have come here and said it's at least two hundred to three hundred years old, and that it smelted gold and silver. The Spanish came down the Conchos from Mexico, then up the Rio Grande on a trade route. The guess is they hauled the ore to the smelter instead of built the smelter near the ore deposits. They did it for the exposed veins of coal, which burns hot, the kind of heat they wanted. They put in coke, then limestone, then gold, and out came the bullion."

SIERRA VIEJA
Coal Mine Ranch, ocotillo plant

Mining titanium is a surer bet. Nelan recently put out bids charging seven dollars a pound to anyone willing to salvage the ruins of a U.S. Air Force B-1 bomber that crashed into the rimrock of the Sierra Vieja while on a six-hour training mission late one night in November 1992.

It is not uncommon for a B-1 to drop below the mountain ridges to practice lowland radar-evasion training flights. The terrain and the dearth of people have, for better or worse, made the Texas Mountains a desirable place for pilots to practice their skills, much to the consternation of ranchers and other folks who live in the mountains to get away from civilization.

Pyote Seven-Zero out of Dyess Air Force Base in Abilene was cruising at a speed of 650 miles per hour when the autopilot was switched off, nine seconds before the B-1 banked and slammed into the vertical sheer rock bluff, the fireball going over the top of the range, destroying the $250 million machine and killing the crew of four. The pilot, who was a last-minute substitute on the mission, was blamed for the catastrophe.

78

"When they saw how hard it hit, and how difficult it was to get in there to the site, the Air Force paid the owners to settle," says Jerry Janosek, one of Nelan's ranching buddies. "It left a smudge on the ridgeline. There's debris a mile wide and a mile and a half from impact, each piece no bigger than a basketball."

Fred Nelan is a fine storyteller. Most of his wilder tales illustrate how life is different under the rimrock. Like this one: "There was a pickup full of wets a couple years back that got stuck in some of that bull dust down on Chispa Road. They called two of their buddies across the river to fetch them out on horseback. While they're trying to pull it out, along comes the Border Patrol in a four-wheel Suburban. They offer to pull out the wets in their truck, but they get stuck in the bull dust too. Along comes another truck, only it's the Marines, who came here to rebuild and improve Chispa Road for the Border Patrol. Well, they get stuck in the bull dust too. The guys on horses eventually pull out the Marines, who pull out the Border Patrol and the wets. Everybody shakes hands and goes on their way. Now, if the wets had a load of pot or a bunch of wets in the back, the Immigration guys would have detained them. But they know how it works down here."

Give us this day, our daily school
—SIGN IN FRONT OF CANDELARIA SCHOOL

JOHNNIE CHAMBERS, the last one-room-school teacher in Texas, is tidying up her stucco-walled home set back from the river road near Ruidosa, her trademark bun perfectly in place atop her head. Beethoven plays on the sound system. Stacks and stacks of books line the walls of several rooms. Paintings and photographs of mountains and the desert adorn the house, alongside several framed panels of arrowheads arranged in circles, stars, and other shapes, and a row of commemorative plates depicting wolves and Indians. One set of photos shows Indian pictographs found on the family ranch. All are handprints except one pair of footprints. "It's the only pair known to history," she says. I know I've never seen a pair before. "Maybe the person didn't have hands," she says. A quilt hangs in the back hallway, each patch a personal thank-you sewn by parents of students of her last class.

I started teaching in Candelaria in 1971. The school in Candelaria is over one hundred years old. There used to be a lot of schools up here—one at Porvenir, one between Candelaria and the ranch, and one at Rancho Viejo. I taught first through third grades at Candelaria. Clemmie Davis taught fourth through eighth grade. I didn't know he was fixing to retire. In 1973, at the end of the school year, I was told the school was all out of money and that everybody needed to find a job. So I drove to Ruidosa to talk to my friend David Fuentes. He gave me a job.

That school was in bad shape—holes in the floor, two outhouses for rest rooms, everything in need of repair. We'd have to drive to the hot springs, which is a fourteen-mile round-trip, every evening to take a bath. I taught down here for four years. We were a common school district. It was not an affiliated school district. Kids that wanted to go to high school had to go to Presidio, and pay tuition. This is a poor area, and most families couldn't afford that.

The Texas Education Agency gave me a choice to teach in Ruidosa, or

Candelaria. So in 1977 I went back to Candelaria. The kids there could go to high school in Presidio if they took the bus from Ruidosa. It was a twelve-mile dirt road from Ruidosa to Candelaria then. That road was bad. The bed was so soft, it got to where you could sink a Volkswagen. One afternoon all the kids and parents loaded rocks in that one hole so cars wouldn't sink in it. For thanks, I had the county commissioner say he was out to get my job because what I did was not school-related.

At Candelaria, I taught third through eighth grade. When I taught at Ruidosa, I did them all—pre-K to eighth. I had anywhere from thirteen to twenty-eight kids. You need a lot of blackboard for that. It keeps you so busy. I think teaching one grade would be boring. It'd of been like going on vacation. They learn so much better together. You have a bunch of little kids; some learn what you're *not* teaching, rather than what you are teaching. Same with those who'd already learned a subject. They were often assimilating what was being taught in other grades. If other kids were using aspects of, say, phonics, it was being reinforced.

I tried to teach them the Three P's: Be punctual, present, and polite. In twenty-eight years, I was never late to school. But sometimes I had to get up at two o'clock in the morning. I'm a punctuality fanatic. When I first taught in Ruidosa, I could tell the students hadn't been taught. I told them I wouldn't accept failure. If the students didn't pass tests, we did them over until we got it right.

I started the Boy Scouts in Ruidosa. At the time, they said women couldn't head up Scouts, but there wasn't nobody else to do it. We couldn't take them to jamborees or they'd find out Johnnie Chambers was a woman. But we took them to a lot of places. Once we camped out at Capote Falls. Kids could have a lot of fun, just to build a fire. I didn't know if they'd like it, being with them from seven to three every day, but they took to it like a duck takes to water.

We always had punishment in school. It's a mild punishment, but in society, they will punish you also, and that's worse punishment than what you get in school. Usually, if one of my students goes to prison, they'll take the GED and they'll write, "Miz Chambers, you were right."

We spoke English. I hadn't been teaching long till this parent came up and said, "My child isn't learning English fast enough." Everyone wrote a slip, saying, "We want our children speaking English only. That's why we send them here. Otherwise, we'd send them to school in Mexico."

I'd hear from school officials maybe once a year. It'd take three hours to get from Presidio to Candelaria back then, and sometimes the road was impassable. We had a principal, I can't remember his name, he said, "Miz Chambers, you ever have disciplinary problems at school, you just call me."

She rolls her eyes. "By the time he'd get here, I'd forget why I called him." She goes on:

I've been evaluated on the last day of school, believe it or not. One superintendent's evaluation was meeting me in a kitchen while he drank a six-pack of beer. He's dead now.

SIERRA VIEJA
ZH Canyon

SIERRA VIEJA
Coal Mine Ranch

You're It. You're the coach, you're the psychiatrist, the counselor, the principal —everything. It's a lot different than city schools. I don't know. The children are so impolite and rude, and of course television doesn't make it any better. My professor at Sul Ross said, "Start out tough, then you can be nice. You can't start out nice, then be tough."

I started giving books to the school, then one of the senators sent us a bunch of books. In the summer, I'd leave books at the store in Candelaria and at the store in Ruidosa. A lot of people started sending us books. We still get them. I just got a box from a doctor and his wife in Austin.

After I retired, they decided it was too expensive to operate the school. Candelaria students are now bused to Presidio, a hundred-mile daily round-trip, the longest school bus commute in Texas.

We've seen a change due to the dope. Nobody used to have to lock your house up. Somebody comes along and was hungry, they'd eat, clean up, and march on. You never left my house without being fed. But the economy in Mexico's gotten so bad, people are desperate to cross. They have two hundred soldiers from Candelaria down to Ojinaga on the Mexican side. They're nice kids, just like anyone else. The only way you're going to solve it, is like liquor—take the money out of it and you solve the problem.

The Border Patrol, used to, it was a game. It wasn't illegal for us to work them. It was illegal for them to work. So they'd play this cat-and-mouse all day, then we'd all go party together at night. It was just a game. Then they passed a law that said we'd get fined for working them. We can't go over anymore, at least legally. They can't come over here and get their mail.

The city scares the hell out of me. There's lots of bad people there. I know what's around me here.

JOHNNIE IS FULLY AWARE of her accomplishments and her sense of place. The certificates of recognition hanging on her wall are the stuff a college president pines for: Who's Who, Outstanding People of the Twentieth Century, Notable American Women. "That's me and the three-star general," she says, pointing to the most recent military commander to hunker down in Candelaria while overseeing improvement of the graded unpaved road on the Texas side of the border. She shows me Douglas Kent Hall's book on the border, in which she's a prominent character. She's on a first-name basis with the Associated Press, all "just because I did something different."

Johnnie's husband, Boyd, lumbers in, stooped over, moving with a shuffle. He sits down, hands on his knees, and his profile turns noble. He's a hardworking man, running horses over thousands of acres of range under the rim of the Sierra Vieja, about as rough as ranch country gets in Texas. It is his chosen life.

Ranching is a tough proposition. We sold all our cattle because the drought got us a little more than a year ago. We drove those cattle over the mountain to the Chillicote Ranch. I guess last year was probably the last trail drive.

Lots of this old country, there's not much grass. Up in the mountains, we've got different kinds of grama. Chino grama is good for horse grazing. Black grama, blue grama, and sideoats grama. All the good gramas are about one inch tall.

A lot of this country under the rim, cattle eat brush and leaves off mesquite. Their beans are good cow feed. Catclaw, they'll eat, Spanish daggers, if you have a lot of blooms, sotol and lechuguilla stalks too. But they've got to be native cattle to feed off that stuff.

I'm too old to get back in the cattle business, even if I wanted to. There's about half as many cattle in this three-county region as there was ten years ago. I don't see much hope for the cow business, or the sheep and goat business. A lot of mountain country is better sheep and goat country. But the price of mohair and wool is terrible.

Predatory animals took over. Predatory animals got so bad, everybody quit fighting varmints. You can't fight 'em alone, if neighbors on either side of you aren't fighting them. We could control bobcat and mountain lion, coyotes too. They stopped us from using airplanes to kill eagles, and the eagles ate us up. You had to poison the eagles before. We used Durham's Red Ant Balls, catching rabbits and soaking them in vats. You'd tie that rabbit to a bush with baling wire. If an eagle ate it, it'd die, couldn't get more than forty feet away. They took all our weapons away.

We used to raise a lot of horses, but mountain lions got to killing our colts. Finally, in '90, I sold twenty mares at one time, kept ten. It got to one year up there, I had this high-powered stud. First colt crop out of that horse, sixteen colts I saw, but lions got ten of them.

For a while, nobody was fighting the lions. It dawned on them they weren't gonna have any deer if they didn't fight the lion. There's an old boy, Henry McIntyre up in Valentine, doesn't do nothing but fight mountain lions. They pay him a salary, and every lion he catches, he gets $250 from whichever ranch he's hunting on. I've known this old boy since he was a boy. I tell you, they got real bad. They raised so many of them in the Big Bend Park, and they killed all the deer there, so they had to go somewhere and eat.

In the daytime, I've seen three lions in my whole life, and a couple more in the headlights at night. I saw one, I got to counting, thirty-nine years ago. I walked into a rockslide. He was sleeping. I nearly stepped on him. He slipped off. I had a .22 pistol. I thought it was probably a bobcat. I shot that lion with the .22. It made him ring his tail and get him moving. That lion left us and went on top of the rim. They caught him a month later. When they skinned him, they found that .22 bullet in his hide. It sure did make him run.

His eyes twinkle at the recollection. "I do like this country."

"He wouldn't know anything else," Johnnie says.

But he does know his chosen way of life is drawing to a close. "You hear of a ranch selling around here, you know good and well it isn't a cow man, because they couldn't afford it. Used to be oil and gas men. Now it's doctors and lawyers. It makes it awfully hard for the ranchers trying to make money from cattle. Big Bend Park, the Tiguas, Big Bend

State Park—they're taking all the land off of the tax rolls. We don't need that stuff. The county will have to raise the taxes of the landowners who are left. And we can't afford it."

As if he ever could.

Theresa Chambers, Johnnie and Boyd's daughter, adds: "When my dad moved down here with my grandparents he said the banks wouldn't even give him a loan. They said that no one could make a living in this old dry country. I moved around some myself, but always knew that I'd be back. I'm home for good now."

KIT BRAMBLETT, who grew up about seventy-five miles upriver from the Chambers ranch, saw the writing on the wall a long time ago: "It's harder to make money ranching for two reasons. The white man committed waste with the land. And the land is overpriced because doctors and lawyers are buying it all up. You can't afford to ranch. That's one reason I became a lawyer at the age of forty."

FIELD NOTES—*Wild Rose Pass. The route from Balmorhea into the Davis Mountains is for me the most visually stimulating entry into the Texas Mountains from the Permian flats. When it rains, the already dreamy landscape turns into a fantasy. After four inches fall in less than a month before the official beginning of summer, the slopes green into a deep emerald beyond recognition. If I didn't know better, I'd think I was in Ireland.*

SIERRA VIEJA
Camp Holland (abandoned fort)

Tourism came to the Davis Mountains when John Robert Prude's family ranch, founded in 1897 six miles west of Fort Davis, began welcoming guests in 1921, making the Prude Ranch the first bona fide visitor attraction in the Texas Mountains. Eleven years later, construction was begun on the seventy-four-mile Davis Mountains Loop (State Highways 118, 166, and 17), an officially designated scenic drive, four years before the white Pueblo-style Indian Lodge and infrastructure for the Davis Mountains State Park in Keesey Canyon was completed by the Civilian Conservation Corps and four years before the dedication of the McDonald Observatory atop nearby Mount Locke in 1939.

Fort Davis, an unincorporated community of some 1,500 residents and the county seat of Jeff Davis County, 5,050 feet above sea level, is Texas's one true mountain town, and, as the gateway to all the attractions mentioned above, the community most closely tied to tourism in the Texas Mountains.

The fort of Fort Davis, a military outpost at the foot of Sleeping Lion Mountain for the Ninth Cavalry and Tenth Cavalry Regiments—the black Buffalo Soldiers brought in after the Civil War to fight Indians and tame the frontier—is a national historic site regarded as the best preserved of all frontier forts in the West and a repository of African American history.

DAVIS MOUNTAINS
Fort Davis National Historic Site

The drugstore lunch counter is reputed to serve the best fountain Coca-Cola in the state. The Hotel Limpia, established in 1912, is the longest continuously operating lodge in the Trans-Pecos. The doll museum is one of a kind. So are the Davis Mountains Environmental Education Center, which works with Elderhostel groups, schools, and organizations, and the Chihuahuan Desert Research Institute, whose arboretum has examples of every tree and shrub that grows in the desert. And there's really no place like McDonald; the popular Star Parties draw more than 150,000 visitors a year to gaze at the heavens, and the Hobby-Eberly telescope is the second largest in the world.

Despite all those points of pride, in 1997 Fort Davis became known to the world for all the wrong reasons. A resident of a box canyon subdivision called the Davis Mountains Resort, twenty miles from the courthouse, had determined that Texas had been illegally annexed to the United States in 1845, declared himself the true ambassador of the Republic of Texas, and seceded from Texas and the United States, designating a small trailer and a lean-to on his land as the republic's "embassy."

This was not so strange considering that one nearby resident had such acute sensitivities to chemicals that he lived in an aluminum house (the Fort Davis area is one of the least polluted parts of the United States) and another, an entomologist, was jailed for illegally smuggling bugs sold by mail order.

But when Richard McLaren and a handful of followers wounded a neighbor and took him and his wife hostage, the Texas Department of Public Safety stepped in, setting up a roadblock at the Pile of Rocks picnic area (where Kit Carson scratched his initials more than a hundred years ago) and attracting one hundred reporters and eighteen trucks with satellite transmitters to beam the breaking story around the world.

McLaren may have been a brick shy of a load, but between the springtime wildflowers and deer and antelope playing in the grasslands during the day, and stars so bright they even outshone the strobing reds and whites of patrol cars and emergency vehicles, he couldn't

DAVIS MOUNTAINS
Cottonwoods along Limpia Creek

have picked a more beautiful place for a standoff. He eventually surrendered and is serving several terms for criminal acts, likely to keep him in jail for the rest of his life.

IF YOU WANT TO KNOW the secret of longevity of mountain people, you might try looking up ninety-four-year-old Lillian "Bit" Miller, who grew up on the officers' line at old Fort Davis and is the oldest resident in the town of the same name. I was going to ask her myself, but on the spur of the moment, she'd left with a friend to take in the symphony in El Paso, almost two hundred miles away.

OF ALL THE JOBS people have in the Texas Mountains, I don't think anyone's is quite as unusual as Jerry W's. Since 1970 he has been shooting laser beams at the moon from atop Mount Fowlkes. As station manager, chief engineer, and assistant project director of the Lunar Laser Ranging project at McDonald Observatory, one of a couple of dozen stations on Earth, he measures distances and elevations on this planet to the most precise degree known to humankind.

"Beaming is a light version of radar," he says. "We use a laser and aim it at one of four targets on the moon—three are American, one is Russian. If we hit reflectors that the astronauts left (they're about the size of an attaché case) it sends the laser beam back to here. We also hit some artificial satellites circling the earth. You want to know where your satellite is? We'll tell you. We're the last living Apollo project left."

When he's not a Light Ranger, Jerry becomes Washtub Jerry, world-famous washtub bassist. Frequently dismissed as a novelty, he takes his instrument seriously enough to tour extensively and perform at cowboy gatherings, and he has appeared on four albums. The Western Music Association honored him as Musician of the Year in 1999. "I grew up in a vacuum of ignorance," he says. "I didn't know the tub was not supposed to be a quality musical instrument. I was a first-chair bassoonist and played accordion. Learning to play the washtub came naturally." As naturally as shooting laser beams at the moon.

"IN THE SPRING OF 1989, the National Park Service announced it was looking at four million acres of privately owned lands in the Davis Mountains for the possible creation of a new national park," says Ben Love, a rancher from Marathon who helped found the Davis Mountains Trans-Pecos Heritage Association, whose green-and-white signs are posted on the gates of many of the largest ranches in the Texas Mountains.

"This ignited a firestorm of emotions among area landowners, many of whom had inherited their ranches from forefathers who had settled here at the close of the Comanche and Apache era in the 1800s. They weren't about to relinquish their lands and heritage, especially to a land-hungry federal government.

"A week after the announcement, ranch owners had a meeting in Marfa. One rancher offered a million dollars as seed money to form an organization to stop the government's encroachment, and the Davis Mountains Heritage Association came into being. The association quickly called for a meeting with the National Park Service at the Catholic parish hall in Fort Davis, attracting a standing-room-only crowd unanimous in their opposition to the proposal. Within forty-eight hours, the proposal was withdrawn.

"Since then, the association expanded its scope to become the Davis Mountains

DAVIS MOUNTAINS
Ash and bigtooth maples

Trans-Pecos Heritage Association, its members representing more than 14 million acres of privately owned lands, with sister organizations in the Texas Hill Country, East Texas, and the High Plains of the Texas Panhandle. Its mission, to maintain the cultural heritage of the region and combat unreasonable governmental intrusions into the private property, remains the same."

"It was about the nicest, most cordial booting out of town I'd ever experienced," remembers Rocky Beavers, one of the Park Service representatives who attended the Fort Davis meeting. He liked the land and the people he met so much, he and his wife, Anna Whit Watkins, took early retirement from the NPS and moved to the Davis Mountains in 1999, where she operates a dressage facility and stables.

With golf courses, condominiums, and developments on the drawing board, the Texas Nature Conservancy moved into Fort Davis after the park proposal was shot down and initiated efforts to preserve open space through conservation easements, a novel concept that offers tax incentives to landowners like Watkins and Beavers who agree not to develop their property. (One rancher and DMTPHA member, exercising his property rights, sold land just south of Fort Davis for a hydroponic tomato farm, a prodigious water user in a water-deprived region and an eyesore that resembles nothing so much as an airport terminal plopped onto the highlands.) By 2000, more than 64,000 acres in the Davis Mountains were protected through easements while the most ecologically fragile area, almost 18,000 acres around Mount Livermore that are rife with endemic flora and fauna—one thousand rare or endangered species all told—was purchased by the conservancy from rancher Don McIvor and officially designated the Davis Mountains Preserve. With the proceeds of the sale, McIvor built a castle on the part of his ranch that he kept.

90

"We realized to be successful, the Davis Mountains project would have to be a private land initiative," says James King, the West Texas director of the Texas Nature Conservancy and a great-great-great-grandson of Captain Richard King, founder of the King Ranch, the biggest, most storied ranch in the state. "We looked at easements as a tool to keep land private, putting restrictions on the property, and using it as a way to maintain the natural resource—no subdivisions, development in concentrated areas, no introduction of exotics. Ben Love and I agree on the endgame. It's how we get there, where we don't agree."

Is it worth it? When James King takes me to Madera Canyon, a spectacular gaping maw rarely seen by the public and one of the most inspiring places I've found in Texas, I figure it may well be.

Bob Eppenauer was one of those ranchers protesting a national park in the Davis Mountains at the town meeting in Fort Davis. He stood up and declared no way would he sell. But he is also contemplating working with the conservancy on an easement so he and his wife, Sheri, can pass the ranch on to their daughter, Dolly Jean, his brother's kids, his cousins' kids. "My deal is first God, then family, then the ranch."

They have survived a seven-year drought by thinking through every purchase. "We ask ourselves, 'Is this something you want, or something you need?'" Sheri says. Now they wonder if they can survive fluctuating cattle prices, estate taxes, the rising value of land for recreational purposes, and other pressures. "I've put a foot in this lifestyle," Dolly Jean says. "But I can't go all the way because I don't know if it'll work."

DAVIS MOUNTAINS
Nature Conservancy preserve
Below Mount Livermore

Bob's idea of a good day is working from four-thirty or five in the morning until nine or nine-thirty at night. He ranches his half of his family's 40,000 acres alone, working the land on horseback because there are no roads. "My granddaddy taught me you can't see a cow in a pickup," Bob says. Sheri teaches school in Marfa, and Dolly Jean runs the family's other ranch south of Marfa and studies natural resource management at Sul Ross in Alpine. "She's a good hand," her father says, paying the ultimate compliment.

Bob has mixed feelings about the conservancy and other outsiders determining what's best for the landowners. "They try to say ranchers can't take care of our land. How do you think those endangered plants survived all those years?"

Whatever the fate of the land, the Eppenauers' ties to it are inviolable. "Last winter, one morning real early, this old cow had this calf just born," Bob says with a faraway look in his eyes. "She was licking it. He got up and wobbled around her foreleg and was about to start nursing. Watching something like that makes it all worthwhile. God had a perfect plan, and if you don't believe that, you're missing something."

DAVIS MOUNTAINS
McDonald Observatory

FIELD NOTES—*Mount Livermore. The trail from Bridge Gap, a saddle ridge within the Texas Nature Conservancy's Davis Mountains Preserve, to the top is the remnant of an old ranch road that extends all the way to the base of the craggy Baldy Peak. The last fifty feet require the agility of a bighorn and enough smarts to know not to look down.*

A marker identifies Baldy Peak, the pinnacle of Mount Livermore, as a United States Coast and Geodetic Survey triangulation station. Three radio towers nearby confirm its stature as the highest point for miles around.

Bumblebees, wasps, ladybugs, and bird droppings are abundant. So are claret cups and DYC flowers—or, as Laurence calls them, "damned yellow composites." A horny toad scurries past. I haven't seen one in the wild since childhood. A pair of peregrine falcons soar above and below Sawtooth, the jagged peak just west of Livermore, joined by zone-tailed hawks and turkey vultures riding the currents, surveying the terrain for rodents and other prey. On a high plateau a good five hundred feet below us, ten javelinas ramble through a grassy meadow.

The white domes of McDonald Observatory, the windmill power farm on a ridge by Bloy's Camp, and the drug blimp, grounded, are easy to spot in the panorama, but in the big picture they are little more than specks.

Thunderheads boil to the southwest and a cool front appears to be moving in from the north, but both systems wash out before reaching us. Instead, a shower falls east of Valentine over the Marfa Highlands, nourishing the grasslands. Off to the north, the Guadalupes are plainly visible. The only sounds breaking the silence are whooshes of wind whipping through the ponderosas and the buzz of winged insects.

Thou shall not speed

—SIGN POSTED AT THE GATES OF BLOY'S CAMP, A COLLECTION OF
METAL-SIDED CABINS ON THE BACK SIDE OF THE SCENIC LOOP

EVERY AUGUST a cowboy camp meeting organized by the Methodists, Presbyterians, and Disciples of Christ draws ranching families from across the Trans-Pecos for spiritual nourishment and socializing, as has been done since 1890. The Baptists have held a similar cowboy camp meeting at the Paisano Baptist Encampment at Paisano Pass between Marfa and Alpine every July since 1914.

"THE MCVAYS ARE land-rich and money-poor," Darice McVay is telling me during a tour of the Red Rock Ranch in the Beach Mountains, just north of Van Horn, one of the only public tours offered on private land in the Texas Mountains. She isn't kidding. The van is a little worn, but the scenery is a visual feast, rich red and warm brown sandstone, bizarrely shaped by wind and water, defying description. Just think of the Beaches as cartoon mountains and listen close to Darice and you'll do just fine.

"The mountains are like clouds. You see in them what you want to. You let your imagination go. That ridge is Camel Ridge. See the camel's face? That's ET under the camel's chin, and that's either Donald Duck or Puff the Magic Dragon. Up here on the left is our Indian satellite dish. I've named this one the Easter Island rock. The wind has eroded these rocks to make them look like they're balanced. Anvil Point, it points due north. And this is Six Mile Mountain—it's six miles from town. It's a miniature of Guadalupe Peak from some angles."

DAVIS MOUNTAINS
Aspens below Mount Livermore

BEACH MOUNTAINS
Movie set, Red Rock Ranch

BEACH MOUNTAINS
Pictograph of deer

Previous pages
DAVIS MOUNTAINS
Mount Livermore

Some of the rocks on Red Rock Ranch are more than one billion years old, among the oldest in Texas. "Precambrian sandstone predates life, and this is one of four natural Precambrian sandstone exposures in the Western Hemisphere. Geologists from UT branches bring graduate students here. They can walk up to a Precambrian exposure, which otherwise should be close to the molten core. Up here, there was a lot of activity that poked this ol' dirt up to the surface."

She shows the earth dam built by the state in 1988, which holds back water from the Sierra Diablo, the Baylors, and the Beaches on those rare occasions when it rains, protecting Van Horn from flash flooding and attracting migratory waterfowl. She points out the Wylie Mountains to the southwest. "The groundcover there is more desertlike," she says, a nice way of saying the creosote, acacia, and yucca are denser here than there. She shows the old Beach homestead, built in 1880, after the nomadic Indians who camped here had been cleared out. She shows grinding holes on a boulder jutting over the edge of a running creek where corn was ground over a period of several thousand years. She takes me up to the Tumbledown talc mine and offers a couple of chunks of the powdery talc rocks to take home. At the adobe village movie set built on a bluff for the television miniseries *Dead Man's Walk,* the prequel to *Lonesome Dove,* she snaps a souvenir Polaroid, placing it in a paper frame that says, "I Was Shot at Anton Chico."

"They spent three months working on it, three weeks filming it, then there's about six minutes on film. And you wonder how these movies could cost tens of millions of dollars."

96

The Texas Mountains make great movie sets. There's another adobe village built for film on the banks of the Rio Grande, west of Lajitas. Once, while driving toward the Davis Mountains from Valentine, out in the middle of nowhere, Laurence and I stumbled upon the ruins of a stucco service station that neither of us had noticed before. A faded Dr Pepper logo was painted on the side. Laurence took a few photos. When I passed through a few days later, I made a closer inspection and realized there never was a there there. It too was a movie set.

NINETY PERCENT of the motels in Van Horn are owned by Indians from India, Darice McVay tells me. There's three different Patels in town, and they're not related, they're from different castes.

McVay sits on the board of the Culberson County museum, located in the old Clark Hotel, where various pioneer families have their own exhibit rooms and the old bar may be the most outstanding artifact. Van Horn existence is all about passing through. The Texas and Pacific Railroad needed a watering hole when the track out west was laid in 1881, and Van Horn had water. Transportation inspired the town's other two museums—the John Madden Haul of Fame at Chuy's Mexican restaurant honoring the former coach and celebrated television football analyst, who travels in a custom bus to games he covers and stops at Chuy's on occasion; and the Smokehouse Auto Museum in the Smokehouse Restaurant, which features a changing display of fifteen classic automobiles from its collection and an extensive array of license plates.

Darice McVay hardly notices when two blimps float past, two of only forty flying dirigibles in the world. The Van Horn airport is a major fueling station for blimps, some of which follow John Madden to football games.

BEACH MOUNTAINS
Hackberry Creek

Jim Daccus waits for me in his pickup on the other side of the gate of the Pezuña del Caballo Ranch in the Delaware Mountains early one afternoon. He's been driving back and forth between this ranch and another ranch that he manages, two hundred miles from here, and he's taken a break to show me around.

Jim is a cowboy. He wears his black wide-brimmed hat pulled low over his brow to shade his face from the sun, which is why cowboy hats look like cowboy hats in the first place. He has a gruff countenance. His salt-and-pepper moustache, the stubble on his chin, and his piercing brown eyes suggest he's not someone to be trifled with, as a fence-cutting trespasser on a four-wheeler on a lark observed when Daccus confronted him. "You scare me," the man told Daccus, about as much of a compliment as he could wish for. His jeans are slick and shiny with dirt and grime. He keeps his spurs on, even when he's not on a horse. He chews Red Man and spits into a plastic Dr Pepper bottle. He's also learned and well read. When Dr. D. J. Sibley, the multi-degreed scholar who owns the ranch and lives in Austin, comes out to inspect the operation, Daccus holds his own in conversation.

But less than five minutes after leaving the highway headed toward the rimrock, Daccus makes a hard assessment of where he fits in the big picture. "We're as relevant to city folks as the Comanches were to us."

Could've fooled me. The cowboy, or vaquero, is the revered symbol of the Texas Mountains, regardless of race, color, creed, or blood; forget the miners, the explorers, the railroaders, the truckers, and the naturalists. He makes his point in a roundabout way, concluding with the public's nostalgia for a time that never was and the growing influence of environmentalists, which gets his dander up. "It's all about control. They want to tell people what to do and how to run their lives."

BEACH MOUNTAINS
Thunderstorm

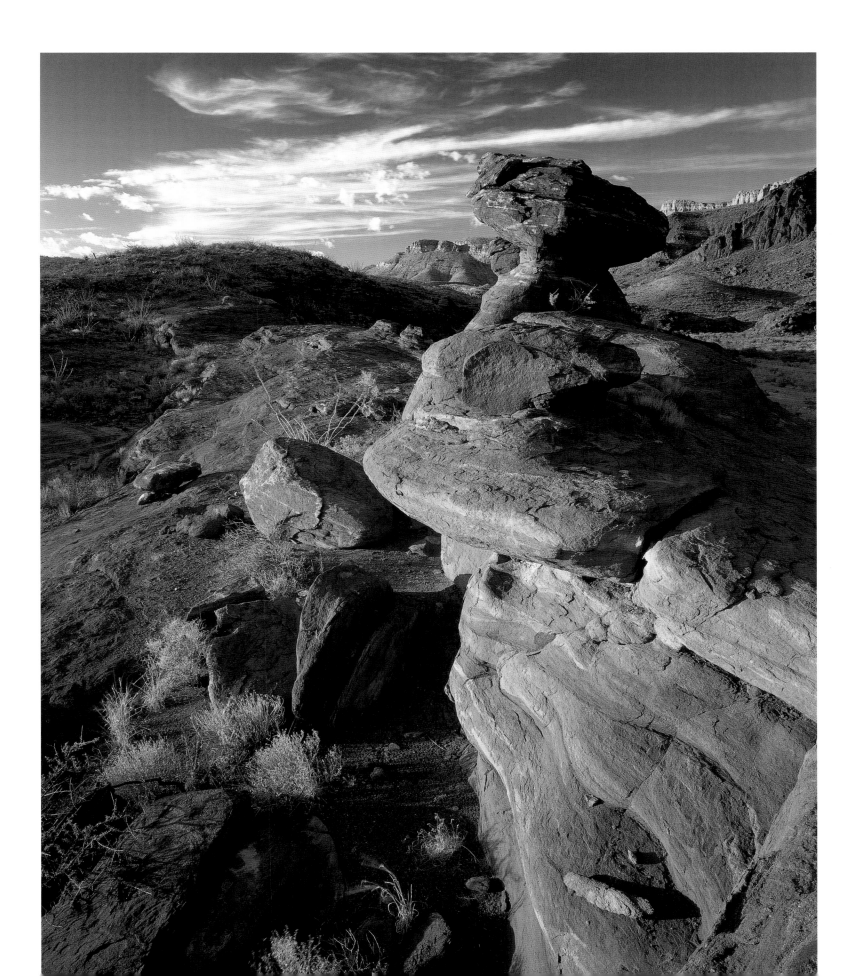

Facing page
DELAWARE MOUNTAINS
View of Guadalupe Mountains

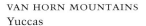

VAN HORN MOUNTAINS
Yuccas

How would they even know how it is out here, he asks? "Some of the biggest mule deer in Texas are on this land. We've put more water here than there ever was in its natural state. How do you explain that to someone who says we shouldn't alter the land?"

He revels in working the ranch solo. His wife lives two hundred miles east, between Alpine and Fort Davis in the Glass Mountains, where he manages the other ranch for Doc Sibley, and she runs her own stock on a third ranch ("She's a good hand," he says). He reads by coal oil lamp. There is no electricity. "You better be friends with yourself," he says.

And friends with the strangers who somehow find their way to the ranch. "There aren't that many wets coming through here. But when they do, I usually give them a ride, knowing they're coming to work up here. It's four days' walk from the river and a day and a half to where they've got work. The wets you find south of Interstate 10 are mostly moving drugs. We call them backpackers. Up here, it's different."

Daccus frequently hosts academics and scientists other than Dr. Sibley. "A lot of geologists come here and look at this. It's like the bottom of the North Sea. Two hundred million years ago, this was fifteen hundred feet under water. I'd settle for three inches of rain right now. Last week when it snowed, there was this fellow here from Nigeria, studying the geology. He'd never seen snow before. We get geologists from Norway, Sweden, England, Ireland, all over."

The Delawares are about as dry as Texas Mountains get. Twelve inches of rain is a wet year. But up top, regardless of the rainfall, the black grama grass grows "stout," as Daccus puts it. The views up top are stout too, with the Sierra Diablo to the west and the Guadalupes, the most majestic of all Texas ranges, dominating the ridgeline to the north and northwest.

Facing page
DELAWARE MOUNTAINS
Windmill power generators

Daccus wanted to make sure I saw what I'm seeing. The Delaware Mountains have been rated as one of the best places in the United States for wind power development. If built out as planned, the thirty-megawatt-capacity Delaware Mountain Wind Farm, presently consisting of forty Zond 750-kilowatt wind turbines 160 feet high, will be the biggest single wind power operation in the United States.

Wind farms are touted as a good thing, "clean" energy that doesn't harm the environment. But for one cowboy in the Delaware Mountains, who has gotten to see the Guadalupes rise above the horizon like the pipes of a mighty Wurlitzer organ whenever he climbs to the ridge, the windmills are a blight, forever sullying the beauty of the land, a blemish that can't be quantified.

Across a fence line, rows of turbines hug the rim, their tri-blade props making a noisy racket. "You ought to stick around 'til dark," Daccus says. Blinking red lights and flashing white strobes are now as much a part of the landscape as sunrise and sunset.

"The neighbors called me when they threw a party, celebrating them going up. I told them, 'I don't feel like it's a reason to celebrate.'"

There's not many places left untouched, he acknowledges. "Everybody wants to find the last best place. Alpine used to be a stock-raising town. Now it's something else. The mystique of the American Cowboy: there's a certain schizophrenia about us now. The people who are moving in, they like the dress, the hat, but the rest of it—I never thought I'd live to be in the time where cowboys and ranchers are villains. They were my heroes. They still are."

DELAWARE MOUNTAINS
Sierra Diablo in distance

FIELD NOTES—*Sierra Diablo, from State Highway 54. After leaving Pezuña Ranch, I drive about ten miles south on Highway 54 toward Van Horn, the Delawares over my left shoulder, looking very different than they did before, older, more alive, their details easier to discern. On my right are the Sierra Diablo, whose slopes continue to intrigue me. I keep slowing down, trying to make out the slot where Victorio Canyon begins, which is hard to see from behind the wheel. Finally I pull over and get out. Beyond the barbed wire fence line I can delineate a dark, narrow crack in the escarpment. This is the spot to which, on January 29, 1881, Texas Rangers chased followers of the Chihenne Apache leader Victorio, the last chief left fighting for his tribe's right to roam Far West Texas, whose tactics have been described as a model for modern guerrilla warfare.*

"My daddy-in-law homesteaded out there in the Diablos in 1908," says Kit Bramblett, an El Paso attorney who ranches in the Eagle Mountains. "That was less than thirty years after the last Indian battle there in Victorio Canyon. The Texas Rangers thought they'd had Victorio's men boxed in there, but they got away, slipping out up a steep draw. The Rangers couldn't follow them because the Indians could just roll a rock down and kill them all. They went back up to the top of the canyon and beat them to Mexico. The Texas Rangers stacked up all the Indians' belongings into a pile and burned it. The remnants of it were still there when my daddy-in-law moved in."

EAGLE MOUNTAINS

The Indians survived in this country as long as they did because they lived lightly on the land and moved around. The fence hugging the road signifies the end of all that. A historical marker in front of the Figure 2 Ranch notes neither the name of the canyon nor the particulars of the fight, only that it was an Indian battle. Instead, the marker sings the praises of the rancher who moved onto the land after the last Indians had been wiped out, listing his civic accomplishments.

And yet, for all the attempts to erase one history, the descendants of the same Anglo settlers who exterminated the Indians tend to idealize them—frequently through arrowhead collections and artwork depicting noble savages on the plains—because, if for no other reason, they managed to live lightly enough on the land to survive for several thousand years. The white man's record of the past 150 years is considerably more checkered.

Which is not to suggest that the natives lived in harmony with the land and each other. The neighborhood turned downright ugly when the Apaches moved into the area, before the Europeans arrived, and exhibited an unfriendly tendency to raid when they were short of supplies. The Comanches followed a century later, making the establishment of any kind of community risky business, since they too embraced the tradition of raiding in times of need, their outstanding horse-riding skills enhancing their efficiency in doing so. It was like having a band of bikers terrorizing your town once or twice a year. The pueblo communities that farmed along the river and the scattered nomadic bands on the desert and in the mountains traded with the Apaches, but were at their mercy too.

Once the Indians were exterminated, miners from California and Alaska moved in. Coronado had entered what is now the United States at La Junta, looking for gold, and Geronimo had said the richest gold mines in the world were in the Guadalupes. Though

104

SIERRA DIABLO
Morning mist

gold was never found, the Hazel Mine discovered near Van Horn in 1856 yielded prodigious amounts of copper and silver through the mid-twentieth century, while the Mariscal, Terlingua, Lajitas, and Shafter mines built an economy in the Big Bend where none had previously existed. Mica, quartz, gypsum, brucitic marble, talc, and crushed rhyolite continue to be mined in the mountains around Van Horn.

I don't hear the ghost cries of Victorio's men when I turn off the engine. I hear the howls of several coyotes, loudly barking and yipping a yip far huskier than a dog's, but no less uninhibited. They're going full tilt in broad daylight. A pair of golden eagles perch close by on two fence posts, watching me but showing no fear of humans. In this wild country, where humans have barely been able to scratch out a living, wildlife rules.

CLAY BREWER, the area manager for Texas Parks and Wildlife's Elephant Mountain and Sierra Diablo Wildlife Management Areas in the Texas Mountains, is one of the few outsiders familiar with the Sierra Diablo. It is remote enough to support desert bighorns, and Brewer is trying to reintroduce the sheep to Texas as part of the state Parks and Wildlife Department's restoration program.

> Existing rock art sites serve as evidence that desert bighorn sheep historically occupied most of the arid mountain ranges of the Trans-Pecos region of Texas. Bighorn numbers during the late 1800s were estimated as high as fifteen hundred animals. By the early 1900s, Texas bighorn populations had declined or were extirpated from much of the historic ranges. By the mid-1940s, the population was an estimated thirty-five individuals. The last documented sighting of a native Texas bighorn occurred in October of 1958 on Sierra Diablo Wildlife Management Area. A number of factors led to the decline: unregulated market hunting, competition for forage with domestic livestock, inability to cope with diseases that domestic livestock carried, and net-wire fencing that restricted movements of desert bighorns.

> We're getting back to the population numbers of the early 1900s. The Trans-Pecos region of Texas currently supports seven free-ranging populations. These occur within the Baylor, Beach, Sierra Diablo, Sierra Vieja, and Van Horn Mountains, and the Texas Parks and Wildlife Department's Black Gap and Elephant Mountain Wildlife Management Areas. Helicopter surveys conducted in August 2000 indicated an increasing population, with 381 sheep observed during 41.9 hours of flight time. The largest population is in the Sierra Diablo. They thrive on the rugged topography, isolation, and the lack of human intrusion. Desert bighorns do not tolerate human disturbance very well.

> Last week I was responsible for the capture and transplant via helicopter of forty-five desert bighorn sheep from Elephant Mountain to Black Gap. This was the largest bighorn transplant in the history of the desert bighorn restoration program.

> Bighorns are a part of the natural heritage of Texas, and we owe it to future generations to make sure that they exist. I am proud to be a part of restoring such a noble animal. At the end of my career, I want to look back and say that I really made a difference.

Facing page
SIERRA DIABLO
Yuccas and piñon pines

SIERRA DIABLO
Piñon pines

The mountains have a way of changing people. I heard a saying once—"Some come planning to change the mountains. The mountains end up changing them." If a person sticks around long enough, they will have no choice but to change here. The McAdoo family is among the last of the original settlers of the Diablo Mountains. Mr. J. V. McAdoo carved out a living for himself, a wife, and four daughters from what many considered to be a wasteland. The remaining family members still involved in the ranches (now split) have it in their blood. The mountains have been part of their lives since the day they were born. I don't know how else to say it except that they have grit. They know how to appreciate the simple things, such as a sunrise and sunset, a good mule, a laugh, or even a warm campfire.

My wife says that I am allergic to people. I like the Diablos because it is sparsely populated and thus lacks the things that come along with people: lights, noise, vehicles, roads, concrete, and Wal-Marts. It wouldn't hurt my feelings in the least to go into the mountains and never come out again.

THOSE WHO MANAGE to live on this land cherish their privacy. The granddaughter of one family got married on the rim of the Sierra Diablo. She had been to college and seen the world, and she invited many of her city friends, some of whom worked for magazines and newspapers, to witness the wedding on the edge of a cliff a thousand feet above a broad basin. Before the ceremony, the bride's grandmother threatened bodily harm to the granddaughter and all in attendance if she saw wedding photos or any photograph whatsoever of this place published anywhere. She wasn't kidding. This was the same grandmother who'd been described to me by a distant relative as rounding up cattle on horseback in the middle of a wind-whipped blizzard, with a bundled baby tethered to the saddle horn.

EVEN IN AN AREA like the Sierra Diablo, people are careful to make the distinction between ranchers and ranch owners as the numbers of the latter grow: a car dealer from Austin, a banker-developer from San Antonio, a lawyer from El Paso, a builder from Austin, a tobacco farmer from Kentucky.

WHEN RAIN COMES, you learn to watch and wait, not necessarily because it is such a miracle to behold since it happens so rarely, but because moisture alters the dynamic of the land so quickly that it too can kill you. That's how it is one afternoon in mid-June, when the monsoon weather patterns are in place to bring afternoon thunderstorms, and curiosity leads me to go from El Paso to Indian Hot Springs downriver.

The first forty miles along the Rio Grande downstream from El Paso are uneventful, since the distance is along Interstate 10, where no surprises are the way it is supposed to be. State Highway 20, with its remnant stretches of what was the old main route before the interstate was built, is more interesting, if you can look past the clutter of strip malls, body shops, bright porta-signs with their flashing lights, and *yonke* yards scattered along the right-of-way. This is the old mission trail, and the missions of Socorro, Ysleta, and San Elceario, established before those in southern California, still stand, functioning as churches rather than as monuments.

Following pages
SIERRA DIABLO
View of Beach Mountains

SIERRA DIABLO

Pecan groves, oversized farm machinery lumbering along the shoulder of the highway, and the broad green valley checkered with fields trick the mind into thinking the Lower Valley below El Paso is really the Midwestern heartland, and the city peels away. Just don't look too far. The desert is less than a mile away.

The landscape turns surreal at the Tiger Truck Stop on I-10, a great big old general store masquerading as a fuel stop whose drawing card, besides being the only gas station between Sierra Blanca and the eastern fringe of El Paso, is a live tiger that is sometimes leashed by the front door. The sign that screams SEE LIVE TIGER isn't kidding.

Right past the Tiger and Fort Hancock, the last in the line of forts that stretched from San Antonio and Fort Worth to El Paso and points west, the road vanishes from the map and the pavement dips and buckles to the point that when a distant shower falls over the Quitmans, the culverts crossing the road rapidly fill with raging flood water.

FIELD NOTES—*Quitman Mountains. The sweetest smell in all of Texas is that of creosote after a rain on the desert in the Texas Mountains. It's a pungent fragrance, almost overwhelming in its aromatic presence, better appreciated knowing how rare rain is, and how it gives life to this severe, forbidding, harsh, desiccated place. The brilliant red blooms that erupt from the tips of ocotillos and the blossoming of a sea of wildflowers tantalize the eye, but the scent is the surest affirmation that the goodness of nature prevails, if only for a few hours.*

This is one of those times when it rains that it just makes good sense to stop and watch, alongside a Border Patrol agent who has done the same. So we talk, about his job, the Border Patrol, and the border. He explains BP politics, how when he was working the area just north of the Rio Grande Valley, agents were apprehending up to six hundred illegals a week, until they were told to quit making arrests. Why? The bureaucrats wanted to show that arrest numbers were down, suggesting that the border was so effectively sealed that Mexicans were no longer trying to enter without papers.

Most of the patrol's presence has been in cities along the border, he said, mainly because that's where the people are and where public perception is formed. But by building a wall in El Paso (within five years of the Berlin Wall's being torn down), the Border Patrol has simply signaled those desiring to enter the United States to move to more remote areas, like where this agent patrolled, to cross. It is, he opines, a silly game.

The border could be sealed, he figures, but at the expense of border jumpers' civil rights—"I mean '*human* rights,'" he says, correcting himself. Citizens have civil rights. You don't have to be a citizen to be covered by human rights.

Aggravating matters has been a campaign to add more agents, since the federal government has increased funding to do so. All well and good, but the increased numbers have lowered standards. Many new agents have no idea where they are or what they're doing.

The rain subsides. We wave adios and go our separate ways.

In the aftermath of the shower, the Quitman Mountains are deceptively lush, shaded as they are by dark clouds and viewed from the level of the river. Up close, they're rocky, barren, downright *mean*, but still fairly awesome.

The road curves and twists and turns through the foothills into some flats, most of

them choked with salt cedar and bogs that emit dank odors. This is where the Rio Grande is least grand, officially designated as a "forgotten river segment" because the narrow, shallow river dries up more often than not, thanks to historic construction of dams upstream and the flourishing of salt cedar, an invader species that has wiped out stands of cottonwood and willow and sucks up what little water is available. It's just as well, in light of the raw waste dumped into the river upstream in Juárez, a city of a million and a half that lacks a sewage treatment plant, and, to a lesser extent, in El Paso.

Here, one hundred miles downstream from El Paso, a white stucco apparition materializes like a mirage on the hot desert river plain. It is very real, however, a thirty-two-room resort hotel built in the 1920s next to a complex of major springs that were known to Indians, gringos, and *mexicanos* alike. Pottery shards indicate extensive relations with tribes of New Mexico and Mexico. Geronimo took the healing waters here after he was "tamed down." The springs were considered so sacred that one day in 1880 when Mescalero warriors saw ten soldiers from the Tenth U.S. Army Cavalry—the black Buffalo Soldiers of the frontier—drinking from the mineralized 180-degree waters, they were so offended by the fouling of sacred waters that the Buffalo Soldiers paid with their lives, or so the story goes.

After the arrival of the white man, the springs were touted as a cure for gout, acne, stomach ulcers, gonorrhea, syphilis, liver disease, arthritis, and a variety of other ailments. John D. Rockefeller, two of the Vanderbilts, and Gene Tunney all sought the cure at Indian Hot Springs. Dallas billionaire H. L. Hunt was so smitten with the descriptions by writer Frank X. Tolbert that he bought the resort. It was the domain for many years of Jewel Babb, the Border Healing Woman.

"We never have any sick people down here except visitors, and they don't stay sick long," Babb told Tolbert in 1966. "We don't have any bad teeth. We don't have any fat folks. If people really knew what we have down here, the bad roads wouldn't keep them away."

The hotel closed down in the 1960s. Jewel Babb moved to Valentine, where she once healed my friend Boyd Elder by rubbing his feet and cured another fellow who Boyd said had been bitten on the penis by a black widow spider. The present owners of Indian Hot Springs, a group of businessmen including a few former legislators, use the lodge, rooms, and bathhouse as a private retreat where everyone lives by a code apart from that of the world beyond the Quitmans.

THE RULES
- *Do not talk politics*
- *Do not talk business*
- *Do not hustle elected officials*
- *Eat when you are hungry*
- *Drink when you are thirsty*
- *Piss anywhere*

JESUS MARMELEJO, the caretaker, shows Laurence and me around, including the corral on a small mesa where the Buffalo Soldiers were slain. The view of Mayfield Canyon from the

QUITMAN MOUNTAINS
Moonset at sunrise

115

corral is a mighty big one, almost 360 degrees. But it wasn't big enough for the soldiers, who died far, far away from home.

I ask Marmelejo about the fallow fields in the river bottom. Was this area farmed? "It used to be," he says. "Then the river went dry and the soil became too salty."

The pumps in the bathhouses are turned off, but Laurence pokes around out back and finds one of the actual springs, a deep hole, maybe twenty-five yards wide, bubbling with clear azure water and lined with luminescent moss. I can't resist. I jump in and tread for about fifteen minutes, as long as I can stand it. For the next three days, I feel no aches or pains whatsoever.

INDIAN HOT SPRINGS is one of three warm springs on or near the river that were commercially developed. Visitors to Big Bend National Park flock to soak in the springs at the ruins of the resort that J. O. Langford dreamed up in the early twentieth century. The old Kingston Hot Springs near Ruidosa, closed to the public in 1990 when sculptor Donald Judd bought the place, then sold after his death, have reopened as Chinati Hot Springs, an alternative, mildly New Age health spa with two indoor baths in converted horse troughs, one outdoor bath, three rustic cabins, a bunkhouse, and a camping area, with twinkling lights everywhere. The caretaker on my last visit was a New England Yankee who'd arrived by train and bicycle from Alpine. Reading materials ran the gamut from *Atlantic Monthly* to *Nostradamus: The New Revelations*.

QUITMAN MOUNTAINS

FIELD NOTES—*Apache Mountains. Hostile, like the Indians who roamed here for six hundred years and were the last tribe left when the white man pushed into this part of the West. Low, dry, and hot, offering little shade or protection from the elements. To the southwest of the range toward Van Horn are fallow fields, a few pecan orchards in perfect rows, and dunes of red sand, remnants of irrigation farming going bust.*

Cattle are rarely seen. Dwellings are practically nonexistent. A big imagination is required to survive on this land, and most often even that has not been enough. The ruins of a gypsum mine, with a railroad spur leading up to it, dust devils swirling around it in every direction, underscore that. The white gyp hills fading off into the east are the last of the Texas Mountains and the beginning of flatland all the way to the Ouachitas. At Dagger Draw on Interstate 10, the Apaches fade into the beginning of the Davis Mountains.

Rusty Wilbanks, a lean and lanky man in his seventies, sits in the back room of the Hudspeth County Sheriff's Office in Sierra Blanca (pop. 700), across the hall from the county jail, less than a mile from Interstate 10, giving me a quick lesson on how area ranchers got so crosswise with government types and environmentalists, whom he disparages as "bunny kissers and tree huggers." It's all about trespassing and lack of respect for private property. "You come onto my land. I don't know who you are. You may say you're Mickey Mouse and you may be Goofy."

Wilbanks runs a ranch in the Quitmans ("They're rough ol' things") when he's not enforcing the law as deputy sheriff (a position he left in early 2001), and he is dressed for either role, in a white shirt with snap buttons and western piping, pressed Wranglers, and tan boots.

Ranching has become a marginal occupation, he says, which is why he works law enforcement too. "Some sell out. Some are still here, like us idiots." I tell him it seems like the only way to be successful in ranching is to be a lawyer. "Oil wells help," he grins. "They make cattle look a whole lot better." But there is no oil to speak of in Far West Texas.

As endangered as it may be economically, ranching still defines social life. "We help each other out. We still do, even if we have to dig a ditch so we can get on our horses, because we're so old and stooped over. It may take a little while longer, but we get it done."

"IT'S A DIFFERENT WORLD out here," George Fore says of Sierra Blanca, referring to both the town and the mountain. "It's *High Noon* all the time."

Being in the middle of nowhere with hardly any people can be both an asset and a liability. The citizens of Sierra Blanca are still trying to decide which. In 1992, sludge from New York City started being hauled to Sierra Blanca by the trainload, destined to be spread over a 40,000-acre ranch north of town.

About that same time, Sierra Blanca was designated by the Texas Legislature as a site to bury low-level nuclear waste from Texas, Vermont, and New Hampshire. A regional coalition of activists and political officials led by a local fellow named Bill Addington raised their voices loud enough, citing loss of tourism dollars and the presence of major geological faults, among other complaints, for the Texas Natural Resource Conservation Commission to cancel the proposed project.

APACHE MOUNTAINS

Addington was shunned by many residents for his efforts, because the cancellation of the project meant the loss of the substantial economic enticements, including a new park, a new fire truck, and the prospect of jobs, that had been offered to this poor, Hispanic-majority community in exchange for allowing the radioactive waste to be buried nearby.

As it is, Sierra Blanca depends on the Border Patrol checkpoint just west of town, the Southern Pacific railroad, the New York sludge ranch, and travelers passing through to keep the tax dollars coming in. Some officials hope for a prison, one of the few growth industries for a small Texas town at the beginning of the twenty-first century.

Sierra Blanca is the easternmost point where green chiles, the essence of New Mexican/Southwestern cooking, are staples on menus, and one afternoon I took advantage of the opportunity to sample them while I met George Fore and Pilar Ortega at a cafe for lunch and a talk.

APACHE MOUNTAINS
Yuccas and sand dunes

Fore, a handsome, weathered cowboy with prominent sideburns, is wildlife manager for La Jolla Ranches. Ortega, a stocky young man in his late twenties partial to gimme caps, is his protégé. George calls him Pilgrim. They used to ranch together. Now Pilgrim's a newly elected county commissioner, a powerful position in Sierra Blanca, and Fore is his advisor. "I knew I could do a better job [than the previous commissioner]," Pilgrim says. "I decided it was God's will. I'm a Christian. I'm a firm believer."

They're talking about how Sierra Blanca Peak, the smooth, pale-colored conical peak that is the most visible landmark between El Paso and Van Horn, got its name. It's Spanish for "white mountain," but beyond that, nobody's sure where it came from.

"Billy Addington used to say it was called White Mountain because it was covered with poppies until the white man came," Fore says. When the white man did come, whatever vegetation was on the slopes was cleared away. Who knows what used to roam there? "I knew a woman who used to live west of the mountain, and she claims her father found a tusk up there many, many years ago," Ortega says.

The two offer to take us around the mountain and show us where the dried and treated sludge is spread, and as we head out they detail other ways the mountain has been exploited. For a short period, beryllium was mined to make nose cones for rockets. In the 1970s, a resort was planned and partially built. There was a restaurant, a dance floor, a landing strip. "They were gonna make it like Palm Springs," Ortega says. The entrance on the south side and the clubhouse, hewn of huge timbers, still stand. The swimming pool is full of dirt. The turf for the golf course was rolled up and auctioned off.

George believes sludge is a good thing. "When Merco [the parent company] started [in 1992], Texas Tech researched its effects. A winter application got a 68 percent increase in forage production within a year. We've had good results. I wish we had enough sludge to do all 150,000 acres of this ranch. We've done about 18,000 acres over eight years. We've got it on 5,000 acres now. When you knock off the greasewood and mesquite, it does even better. The Tech researchers told me that all the creosote and mesquite didn't develop over time, that it was an episodic event from the drought of the 1950s, that's when it took over.

"I really would like to see it get bigger," Fore says. "We've got lots and lots of land that could benefit by that. After the second year of application, antelopes started showing up." Ortega runs down the wildlife inventory—pronghorns, mule deer, coyotes, mountain

SIERRA BLANCA
View from Quitman Mountains

SIERRA BLANCA
Ocotillo plants and prickly pear cacti

lions ("Lots, they're a problem for us"), blue quail, all sorts of migrating birds, bobcats, badgers, raccoons, ringtails, javelinas, way too many rabbits, prairie dogs (one town is on the application site), and enough mice and rodents to attract eagles and hawks.

It's really hard to tell if sludge is a good thing or a bad thing. For all the talk how it'll green up the desert, there's been too little rain to see the difference. And I keep thinking about an acquaintance in Van Horn who swears a doctor there has identified a strain of flu infecting locals that is found nowhere else but New York.

But sludge is almost minor compared to what a mining company is doing, gouging out the north face of the peak, extracting hard rock for railroad track ballast. "They don't have any mitigation, reseeding, or restoration going on," Fore says when he points it out. "They'll gouge it until the economics say quit. Apparently, you've got a company whose interest in land doesn't go beyond crushed rock."

At least the "Poo-poo Choo-choo" provides forage for cattle, when it does rain. That scar will be forever.

"IN WEST TEXAS, if it does not stick you, sting you, burn you, or bite you, it's a rock." That's what it says on James Schilling's business card for the Sierra Motel, established 1939, a charming rock-walled motor court near the highway in Sierra Blanca that he acquired in 1999. Schilling, who has worked on ranches in the Texas Mountains for much of his life, is restoring the motel, betting he can pull a few more travelers off the highway.

He's got more going for him than he realizes. The motel's architecture is quite appealing, and Sierra Blanca has a rich past to talk about. The silver spike that linked the Texas and Pacific and the Southern Pacific railroads was struck here on December 15, 1881, completing the second transcontinental rail line in America, according to a marker on a traffic island by the main intersection.

Another marker details an equally noteworthy event a year and a half before the silver spike was driven. General J. J. Byrne, a surveyor, was killed in one of the last raids by Apaches, led by the warrior chief Victorio, fifteen miles south of here at Quitman Pass.

Quitman Pass is the only break in an otherwise continuous thirty-mile ridge that defines the Quitmans. It's one of the least vegetated mountain ranges in Texas, and not particularly overwhelming at first sight, but its presence has influenced transportation routes across West Texas since humans first passed through the area.

James gives ranch and birding tours, which means that for a price he'll take visitors to the top of the Eagle Mountains, about ten miles east of Sierra Blanca and two hours up a freshly cut gravel track that requires four-wheel drive and steely nerves.

FIELD NOTES—*Eagle Mountain. The peak is at least 7,340 feet above sea level, according to James's altimeter watch, and the highest point outside the better-known Guadalupes, Chisos, Chinati, and Davis ranges. It feels like high country. "There's elk up here," James says, and we wander through lush grasses, oak, juniper, and alligator juniper.*

The views are wondrous. To the south, ragged, torn-up slopes and a sawtooth ridge tumble all the way to Mexico. The Davis range and the Viejas bulge up to the east. The Quitmans spread southwest toward Mexico and the Pacific. Sierra Blanca and Little

Sierra Blanca dominate the horizon toward El Paso, both of them whiter than the other slopes. The Diablo plateau lifts higher and higher eastward until it tops out at the escarpment ridge of the Sierra Diablo, where the land drops precipitously to the Delaware basin. Behind the Diablos rise the Guadalupes; in front of them the lower swells of the Devil's Ridge trail toward the interstate and the railroad, which look close enough to touch, the tiny toy line of trucks, like motorized wagon trains tracing the old San Antonio–San Diego Jackass Mail stage route, constant to the vanishing point.

Though I've driven this route dozens of times, until Bill Addington pointed out the Eagles and James Schilling took me up top, I had no idea the Eagles even existed.

The view into the valley of the Rio Grande and Mexico explains the huge forty-foot globe near the top of Eagle Mountain, surrounded by a chain-link fence topped with razor wire, another genuine Texas Mountains incongruity. According to a posted sign, it is a radar dome built by the Federal Aviation Administration in 1996 for air traffic control. But everybody around seems to know this is radar intended to monitor illegal flights trying to sneak across the Rio Grande. On the other side of the radar is another road, paved and with guardrails, built by taxpayers for $13 million, though only authorized personnel may drive it. I get the sense that at least two landowners in the Eagles don't get along.

Of course, neighbors and neighborhood are relative in the Texas Mountains. Topper Frank, who ranched more than 40,000 acres in the Sierra Diablo until he packed up his family and moved to Argentina in 2001, left because, as one acquaintance put it, "He thought West Texas was getting too crowded."

Charley King, the foreman of several ranches, including Topper Frank's old place, says Topper wrote him a letter recently and said it rains thirty inches a year in Argentina. "It hasn't rained thirty inches in ten years here," Charley grins.

Charley is accustomed to this big country. He refers to a thirty-section ranch, almost 20,000 acres, as "a real small place." He knows it takes a lot of land to run cattle. "Shoot, in Argentina you can put one cow on every five acres. That's a lot better than here." And he's a realist when it comes to moisture and the lack thereof. "People around here say it's got to rain. Well, it doesn't if God doesn't want it to."

One of the spreads Charley runs has a forest of Faxon yucca, the largest species found in Texas, which is one of the more bizarre landscapes in these parts. The owner, who insists on anonymity, lets a nursery from Albuquerque harvest a truckload every six months or so. The ranch also augments its cattle operation by renting space for cellular towers and radio antennae on the ranch's upper ridges, and through hunting leases. Hunters seeking to bag the grand slam of mountain sheep are willing to pay $40,000 and more to hunt desert bighorns up in the high country, which rises to 6,442 feet above sea level.

ONE OF THE BEST-KNOWN characters in the Texas Mountains is a woman called Burro Annie, a familiar figure especially around Sierra Blanca, Van Horn, Valentine, and Marfa. She's usually leading her burro on long walks by the road, or sometimes sleeping under an improvised tarp, often in the heat of the day, and she occasionally drives a Cadillac that pulls

Facing page
EAGLE MOUNTAINS
View southeast from summit

a trailer. No one is sure what her real name is. She does not engage in conversation with strangers. It is said she is a woman of some means—her family sends her money when she needs it—and that hers is a chosen life.

One night, in a pizza parlor in Sierra Blanca occupied by two Latino men, a writer and a photographer, a man with a scruffy beard, and an elegantly dressed woman wearing a scarf, Burro Annie appeared at the door like an ethereal spirit conjured from the mist. She ordered a pizza. No one stopped and stared, no one said a thing. When her order was served, she vanished into the night.

The next morning, James Schilling at the Sierra Motel told me the man with the beard and the woman with the scarf were Swiss Italians passing through. She told him she and the boyfriend had been traveling through the Southwest for two weeks and finally, right here in Sierra Blanca, they saw what they'd come looking for—the America of big skies, big land, and endless horizons that they'd always heard about. James may be on to something.

FIELD NOTES—*Guadalupe Mountains. Best appreciated from Dell City, where groundwater has turned the desert into rich, lush, productive farmland, and fields of red chiles and the small hill with the white letters* DC *painted on its slope provide a most splendid foreground: Guadalupe Peak rises above the other promontories on the ridgeline like a point on the icing of a multilayered cake or the choppiest wave on a mountain sea. The southern half of the ridgeline is defined by an exposed face where a light show eternally plays.*

Texas's tallest mountain suffers an inferiority complex, situated as it is behind El Capitan, whose dramatic prowlike face thrusts 2,000 feet above the alluvial plain and sometimes obscures Guadalupe Peak altogether.

The view from outside the offices of the Hudspeth County Herald *in Dell City is fairly remarkable, especially with a light dusting of snow on the upper slopes. "It's sacred to me," Mary Lynch, the editor, says wistfully. "I just think it's beautiful."*

"WHEN I MOVED BACK to the Salt Flats (near the Guadalupes) in '54, I used to visit a white-haired old man who lived in Pine Springs named Uncle Ben," recalls El Paso county attorney Kit Bramblett.

Now Uncle Ben was a character. If he did all the things people said he did, he'd of been at least 150 years old. Kids would be coming through Pine Springs all the time in the summer, and if they'd stop and talk, he'd tell them he knew where there was buried treasure. They'd all go up to where he said there was buried treasure and dig and have a party until the beer ran out.

About 1960, old Uncle Ben got some college kids from Rutgers all worked up, convincing them there was buried treasure. They dug a hole about twenty feet deep until they wore out, quit, and left. Me and Mr. Brown saw where they were digging and got a box and dropped it in the hole, covered it up, but left it so part of a corner was sticking out. Then we went and told Uncle Ben that Mr. Davis from the gas company had found the buried treasure the kids had been digging for. Uncle Ben went and saw it, discovered the box was empty and got all fussed up, and went to

Facing page
GUADALUPE MOUNTAINS
Guadalupe Mountains National Park
El Capitan and Guadalupe peaks

Mr. Davis's door. We heard him yell, "You goddamn son of a bitch claim jumper, I want my money!"

Some years before that, Uncle Ben was talking to me. He had this cave needle, he said. This cave needle could divine caves. He told me, "On that hill over there, I've divined there's a cave. Geronimo has buried a bunch of treasure from the Diablo mine there." I said, "Ben, show me where it is. I'll go over there and dig it up." He said, "Son, if I showed you, you wouldn't know how to spend it. The wealth would ruin you." I went over the next day and when I came back, I said, "Ben, I found it. I saw it and covered it up, so no one will find it. I couldn't show it to you, because that wealth would just ruin you." He glared at me and said, "You're just a smart-aleck S.O.B."

My favorite mountains are probably the Guadalupes. Judge Hunter owned those mountains, bought it at six, seven dollars an acre, sold it for forty-seven dollars an acre. I remember when they were talking about making the Guadalupes a national park. Ol' Ben said that goddamn park won't be nuthin' but a lion's den. He was right. There's no deer in the park. There's no deer anywhere. I can show you lion prints on the east side of the slope. You can't kill a lion over in Guadalupe Mountains National Park. All the deer and elk there are gone because they let the mountain lion go. The superintendent there says they've got four lions in the park. Bullshit. They've got forty.

Every time I'd go out to punch cows, round up horses, I'd carry a gun. I wanted to see a lion. I finally did when I was forty-nine years old. I was in the Eagles by Oxford Canyon, slick rock country, and about ten or twelve feet from me, there's a lion in the tree. He jumped out of the tree and ran. I was on a fairly young horse, and when that lion jumped out of that tree it spooked him. I was just barely able to not end up on the ground. I was sitting on my hands, but when I went after him he turned up the side of the hill. I let him get thirty, forty yards up the bush and took aim. The first shot I got off, I shot his tail off. But I couldn't get him up there. Got some dogs and eventually got him. He's lying up there on the bed of my wife's house now.

That damn communist.
> —ONE RANCHER'S ASSESSMENT OF THE LATE SUPREME COURT JUSTICE
> WILLIAM O. DOUGLAS, WHO PUSHED FOR NATIONAL PARK PROTECTION
> FOR THE GUADALUPE MOUNTAINS AND SEVERAL OTHER
> FRAGILE ECOSYSTEMS IN FAR WEST TEXAS

THE GUADALUPES OPENED as a national park in 1972 with more than half of it (46,850 acres) designated a wilderness area six years later, meaning there are no visitor facilities other than rest rooms and primitive campgrounds. A hiker's paradise with more than eighty miles of trails through desert and coniferous forest, it is as it was when the first explorers entered the area—spartan, wild, and windy.

How windy? As Fred Marshall, the natural resources program manager of Guadalupe Mountains National Park, says, "You know it's windy when . . .

Guadalupe Mountains National Park
Gypsum dunes

- Employees park all vehicles facing west to keep the doors from being sprung on their hinges.
- During a wildfire you think you're being hit by firebrands but you discover they are wind-blown rocks.
- Unoccupied tents and tent trailers in the campground become airborne.
- You trip yourself in a crosswind because your uplifted leg is blown in front of the other one.
- You are fearful of hiking with a large-profile backpack because the wind can blow you off the trail.
- You see two-foot-diameter trees blow over or snap off.
- The weather vane and anemometer are blown off the weather station.
- A thirty-six-foot motor home parked in the campground is picked up and laid on its side.
- Eight-and-a-half-inch tubular steel towers at the nearby wind power plant are bent and blown over (I seem to recall that event was 163 miles per hour)."

FIELD NOTES—*Top of Guadalupe Peak. Touching the roof of Texas is a heady sensation, unlike climbing any other Texas mountain. When seen from above, El Capitan is more connected to the rest of the ridge, the Delawares worn and wrinkled, the white gypsum dunes at the base of the western flank to the west rendering the landscape lunar, but hardly stark.*

Have you ever looked down *on a rainbow? I have.*

Summiteers from five to seventy have written rather eloquently about feeling closer to God, about a rattlesnake sighting on the trail delaying their ascent. Several object to the squat aluminum pylon at the summit emblazoned with the logos of the U.S. Postal Service and American Airlines. Blowing up this ugly sculpture, one climber writes, "would be something special in the air."

GUADALUPE MOUNTAINS
Guadalupe Mountains National Park
Smith Spring

Facing page
GUADALUPE MOUNTAINS
Guadalupe Mountains National Park
El Capitan Peak, from Guadalupe Peak

I absentmindedly pick up a piece of rock. It is calcium carbonate—limestone—embedded with the fossils of hundreds of tiny clamshells. Once upon a time, the highest point in Texas was under the sea.

McKittrick Canyon harbors a herd of Rocky Mountain elk brought in by Judge Hunter in the 1920s after the native herd was hunted out, a four-mile trout stream, and the greatest variety of vegetation for a hundred miles in any direction, the latter attribute attracting hundreds of weekend hikers who are willing to walk at least six miles in and out of the canyon every October and November. Their reward is the most intense display of fall colors in Far West Texas. It's not quite Vermont, but pretty darn close.

New water wars on the horizon; get ready to fight
—HEADLINE IN *Hudspeth County Herald*, NOVEMBER 10, 2000

We're saving water for America's future.
—RADIO COMMERCIAL FOR EL PASO WATER UTILITIES,
KROD-AM, EL PASO, NOVEMBER 11, 2000

Valley of the living waters
—BILLBOARD ON THE DELL CITY AG LOOP,
LEADING INTO DELL CITY FROM U.S. HIGHWAYS 62-180

"EVERY DESERT CIVILIZATION failed because of water," Jim Daccus tells me. "This land is not able to support large populations, and no single government entity has been able to control it."

ONE FALL DAY, state representative Pete Gallego, whose district covers 34,000 square miles—almost all of the Texas Mountains—drove up with an aide to Dell City for a noon enchilada lunch at a small cafe sponsored by the Dell City Chamber of Commerce. The chamber members, and almost everyone in town, were worried about a feasibility study being made to build a pipeline from Dell City to El Paso, to meet that growing city's need for drinking water, at the expense of irrigation farming around Dell City. With the Rule of Capture governing groundwater law in Texas, meaning a landowner can pump all the water they want beneath the land that they own, Gallego couldn't promise the gathering that El Paso wouldn't suck Dell City dry, but he was clearly heartened by what he saw as a unified front among rural interests.

"For the first time in my life," he told the gathering of twenty-five, "Culberson, Hudspeth, Presidio, Jeff Davis, and Brewster counties are singing from the same hymnbook. As far as I'm concerned, Texas was built on a rural economy that was the backbone of the state for many years, and we can't turn our backs on that because the computer companies and the high-tech industry have moved in. We have to make sure the economy includes farming. You all live out here for the same reason I live in Alpine. We have chosen to live a more perfect way of life, and I'm not willing to give that up. As long as I'm in the legislature, that will be my attitude."

Facing page
GUADALUPE MOUNTAINS
Guadalupe Mountains National Park
Williams Ranch

After the lunch, Gene Lutrick, the chamber president, bragged that Dell City has the best fishing in the United States: "A thousand miles in any direction is great fishing."

DISTANCE TAKES A DIFFERENT dimension in the Texas Mountains, as does language, Kit Bramblett explains to me one day: "I talk Spanish like I talk English. The only people I spoke English to was my mama and daddy and my grandmother and my granddaddy. Back when I was going to school, Mexicans would get whipped for talking Spanish in school, but I've been whipped more than any Mexican for talking Spanish on the playground.

"My wife grew up in the Sierra Diablo. For twenty years, she and I lived up at the base of the Guadalupe Mountains.

"When I was a little kid, I'd go stay with my uncle in the Cornudas. I grew up like Charles Goodnight, on a horse. You couldn't lose me. I could look at the stars and the sun and by God, I couldn't get lost. If there was a dust storm, where you couldn't see the sun or stars, I had the good sense to sit until it subsided. The only time I got lost was visiting an uncle up in Boston, and going hunting in Maine. I couldn't read trees and there were too many of them. I can get lost, but not here."

GUADALUPE MOUNTAINS
Guadalupe Mountains National Park
McKittrick Canyon, historic line cabin

Facing page
GUADALUPE MOUNTAINS
Guadalupe Mountains National Park
McKittrick Canyon Creek

FIELD NOTES—*Cornudas Mountains. A moonscape dominated by three sugarloaf peaks, the top half of one blown off like Mount Saint Helens, only a few million years earlier.*

STRADDLING THE TEXAS–NEW MEXICO LINE, the Cornudas Mountains are easily overwhelmed by the grandeur of the Guadalupes to the east and the buzz factor that the Huecos generate from pictographs and rock-climbing activities. All of the range is privately owned. Its taller pinnacles are in New Mexico. Most of what's in Texas looks like dry rubble. Trees are nonexistent on the slopes. The grasslands surrounding the mountains are permanently stressed and worn out, marginal before they were even grazed. Creosote, cholla, yucca dominate the landscape, a few hedgehog and strawberry cactuses, broomweed at the edge of the road, and occasional thickets of mesquite in the draws adding some color.

Laurence has a special place in his heart for the Cornudas. He roamed around the range in his younger years. He wants to show me a place he remembers, so we veer off the highway, down long stretches of rough dirt roads, and park in the literal middle of nowhere. Then we hike a while, toward a low, tilted peak called Sierra Diablo with boulders scattered around its base, a small mountain that becomes larger and more impressive the longer we move toward it across the open flats under a blazing sun. Viewed from the proper angle, it suggests the Rock of Gibraltar.

This is difficult country to trespass on, Laurence remarks as we walk in the heat. Every vehicle leaves a voluminous trail of dust in its wake, visible for miles. I'm comforted that he has received permission to be where we are.

Up close, some boulders are more than twenty feet high, sizeable enough to provide shelter and shade on this treeless plain in dire circumstances. I'm not the first one to reach this conclusion. One jumble shows plenty of evidence of previous occupation. Middens of heat-cracked stones used in cooking pits are scattered about. Piles of flint shards are on the shady side of boulders. And finally, what Laurence remembers from twenty years before: two crude petroglyphs etched into the granite, barely visible, both square patterns with squiggly lines, one like a labyrinth, the other a cosmic inner curl. Probably nothing more than something to do while passing the heat of the day in the shade, I guess. But an etching that's lasted longer than the artist might have anticipated.

Mary Foster lives and ranches in the Cornudas. The blue-eyed blonde with a sunny disposition holds a second job at the Cornudas Cafe (pop. 6), the one genuine roadside attraction between the Huecos and the Guadalupes. Gimme caps hang from the ceiling. License plates cover the walls. Autographed napkins underneath clear plastic cover the tabletops. The green chile burgers are famous. Mary always keeps the jug-size glasses of ice tea filled.

Most of her adult life has been spent on a ranch or in Dell City, so when the subject of the city of El Paso coveting Dell City's irrigation water, her sunny disposition turns sour. "I grew up in El Paso," she says. "But I don't like to go to the city anymore. My daughter goes shopping for me. I like it out here. It's quiet. It breaks my heart if all our farms and ranches go. Where will people get their food?"

CORNUDAS MOUNTAINS, SIERRA TINAJA PINTA
Cerro Diablo Peak

CORNUDAS MOUNTAINS, SIERRA TINAJA PINTA
Cerro Diablo Peak

FIELD NOTES—*Hueco Mountains. Rising out of the desert llano east of El Paso, the Hueco Mountains are noteworthy for their tanks, or small natural basins that collect water; They're historically the most reliable source for the 150 miles between the Guadalupes and the Franklins. Cerro Alto, 6,787 feet above sea level, dominates the range, high enough for its peak to be obscured by low clouds on occasion.*

Lesser rises give the Huecos their character, justifying the state historical park designation for 860 acres in 1969 as a means of protecting one of the most extensive arrays of pictographs found anywhere—modern graffiti artists were tagging over graffiti left hundreds and thousands of years ago—and drawing climbers to scale rocks rife with natural "jugs" for handholds and footholds that are rivaled only by boulders in Fontainebleau, France.

The range is also the eastern border of miles of lines etched into the desert sands that, from the air, are as mysterious and unfathomable as the Nazca lines on the Peruvian desert. They're actually leftovers of a scam in which developers sold land for five dollars an acre to people far away who never saw what they were buying. Even with the expense of blading the network of roads and cul-de-sacs, there was considerable money to be made from the small payments. But few people ever moved here, mostly because of the lack of water and electricity.

The desert hills around the Huecos are so bare and lightly vegetated that the layered bands of sediment marking millions of years are clearly visible, as are the ill-fated subdivision plats and the scars and gouges made by stone and rock quarries, one of the few means by which humanity has been able to exploit this harsh land.

To reach the Huecos, one must leave U.S. Highways 62-180, turning north at the Hueco Mountain Estate land sales office, which resembles a UFO.

The mobile homes, the geodesic domes, the flimsy, duct-taped walled compounds fall away the farther north you go into the Hueco Valley. The boulders get bigger and bigger.

HUECO MOUNTAINS
Hueco Tanks State Historical Park, pictograph

North Mountain, a 150-foot jumble of igneous rock boulders thirty million years old sitting on a sedimentary bed near the park entrance, is the climbers' holy ground. During the mild winters, from November to March, they converge here from all over the world to practice technicals and avoid cratering or getting decked on the massive outcroppings, before tackling larger faces elsewhere during the summer.

But the same rocks have art dating back several thousand years, and restrictions imposed in 1998 to discourage defacement of pictographs have cramped the climbers' ability to climb and sent the annual visitor count plummeting from 75,000 to 17,000 in less than five years.

An unusual alliance has since formed between the rock climbers and the Tigua Indians of El Paso, who observe seasonal ceremonial rites in the Huecos and want to take over stewardship of the park from the Texas Parks and Wildlife Department.

Hostilities between climbers and park rangers have grown more pronounced, as reflected by a posting on an El Paso climbers' Web site, venting about the closure of areas like Bucket Roof, Nuclear Arms, Blood and Gore, Artist's Opposition, and Saint Vitus

HUECO MOUNTAINS
Hueco Tanks State Historical Park
East Mountain

Dance: "Isn't it sad how all those tree-hugging, rock-art worshipping, lichen licking fascists who think YOUR [*sic*] presence in the park is so damn harmful—isn't it tragic how rarely they show up to appreciate the place they have 'saved'? Those of us who love Hueco for what it is—beautifully-shaped rocks—are banned. The tallies for 'guided tours' for 1999 were interesting—117 for climbing, vs. a handful for other activities."

Climbers, Tiguas, and aficionados of pictographs aren't the only ones to covet Hueco Tanks. Gutzon Borglum, the sculptor who created Mount Rushmore, once contemplated his own giant-sized Rushmore-esque pictograph carving there, as well as one for Santa Elena Canyon in the Big Bend. He also proposed a Robert E. Lee statue for Fort Worth, and a Christ statue in Corpus Christi. But when he was denied the commission to do the Alamo cenotaph in San Antonio, he left Texas and eventually made his way to South Dakota.

11,594 Aliens
9,154 lbs of narcotics
—STATISTICS FROM THE POSTED TOTE BOARD DETAILING SEIZURES MADE
AT BORDER PATROL CHECKPOINT NEAR THE HUECO MOUNTAINS
ON U.S. HIGHWAYS 62-180

HUECO MOUNTAINS
Hueco Tanks State Historical Park
West Mountain

FIELD NOTES—*Westbound on Interstate 10 toward El Paso. From a distance, the Franklins are little more than three left-sloping flanks, a smaller rise behind them to the north, barely bulging above the flat horizon line and the vanishing point at the end of the highway, the mountains deep blue, dark, and mystical, the sky a pale aqua, flecked with soft pinks, deeper hues of burnt orange and blood red, bleaching into white in retreat from the advancing night.*

Dr. Phil Goodell, geology professor, University of Texas at El Paso:

In the Guadalupes, you get these big reefs up top and this big basin to the south. The topography is like an ocean three hundred million years ago. It's like Mecca for anyone interested in geoscience. But the Franklins are great to study, too. You can start on Alabama Street on the east side of the mountain and walk to Scenic Drive—it's like walking through geologic time. The Franklin Mountains have the oldest rocks. They're from a period of older-than-old time, Precambrian, 1.1 billion years old. And that's the top of the mountain. Structurally, this is the highest mountain in the state of Texas, with the oldest rocks on top of the mountain, not the bottom. It's just weird. The tilt you can see from south of the range results from the western side moving downward and the eastern side moving skyward.

There hasn't been an authoritative geologic map of the Franklin Mountains. It's one of the last ranges left in the United States that is unmapped. It's very complex. One geologist started mapping it in the sixties and he committed suicide. Everyone knows about Carlsbad Caverns. What about the Caverns of El Paso? We have all this limestone. Twenty years ago the city street department was digging up on Murchison Street and twelve feet down, the floor fell through this trench they were digging. They were digging through this cavern.

There's all these old stories about Spanish gold, treasure, mines in the Franklins. Stand at Guadalupe Church in Juárez in late January at sunrise and look for shadows on the hillside of the Franklins. It's supposed to direct you to a mine.

La biblia es la verdad, leela (The Bible is the truth, read it)
—MESSAGE PAINTED ON WHITEWASHED ROCKS ON THE JUÁREZ MOUNTAINS,
CLEARLY VISIBLE FROM SCENIC DRIVE AND MOST OF EL PASO

NAMED FOR EARLY ANGLO settler Franklin Coons, the Franklin Mountains are Texas's urban range, surrounded as they are by El Paso. The southern end of the Franklins descends into the heart of El Paso, and the proximity to the city gives the range its distinguishing features: Scenic Drive, the most breathtaking vista found in a Texas city, overlooking El Paso and Juárez beyond—two cities, three states, and two nations in one view; homes climbing up the eastern and western slopes; television and radio towers hugging the ridgeline at the top, with an aerial tramway running up to Murchison Peak; the lighted star at the southern base; the fading *E* and *C* letters painted in white on the upper slopes, part of a longtime mountain tradition; and Trans Mountain Road, the highway route through the heart of the range, crossing the historic Smuggler's Pass.

Facing page
FRANKLIN MOUNTAINS
Franklin Mountains State Park
View from North Franklin Mountain

The Butterfield Overland Stage route, which revolutionized intercontinental transportation when it was launched in 1858, passed the base of the Franklins on its way from Tipton, Missouri, to San Francisco during the heyday of the stagecoach. The twelve-hundred-mile journey took fourteen days. Today, a commercial jet travels the distance in a little more than two hours. The first lighted air beacon between the Mississippi River and the West Coast was erected on Murchison Peak in 1928.

"I WAS THE FIRST PERSON to ride Trans Mountain on a bicycle," says Joe Christie, the former state senator from El Paso. "The road hadn't been dedicated yet. But I got on my bike and rode it anyway." Christie is responsible for pushing the creation of the 24,247-acre Franklin Mountains State Park, the second-biggest state park in Texas and the largest urban wilderness in the United States, through the Texas Legislature in 1979, in response to activists led by John Sproul and the Franklin Mountains Wilderness Coalition, a citizen pressure group formed to stop urban sprawl creeping up both slopes of the range and thwart the plans of developer Dick Knapp, who had platted out much of the mountains as subdivisions.

The most visible parts of the park are areas bordering Trans Mountain Road, the thoroughfare through Smuggler's Pass that connects northeast El Paso to northwest El Paso, and the small area adjacent to McKelligon Canyon, on the eastern slope near the tramway. The heart of the park, the Tom Mays Area, with campgrounds, rest rooms, showers, interpretive exhibits, and trailheads to the upper slopes, including North Franklin Mountain, the highest peak in the range, is tucked away off Trans Mountain Road a couple of miles from Canutillo.

"It's mainly for the outdoor enthusiast and backpacker," says Ray Sierra, superintendent of Franklin Mountains State Park, a nice way of explaining the Franklins aren't for everybody. Two hundred people make for a busy weekend, or one for every thousand acres or so. Sierra considers the park to be crowded on rare occasions such as during the Coyote Classic Mountain Bike Race in February. "Our problem is exactly the opposite of most parks," he says. "We need for folks to know about us, market the place, let people know we're here."

Every October, El Paso stages a Celebration of Our Mountains festival, the only festival in Texas specifically honoring the state's mountain heritage. On the last Sunday of October, 35,000 pilgrims climb a two-and-a-half-mile switchback trail toward a 42-foot-tall limestone statue of Jesus at the top of Mount Cristo Rey, the point where Texas, New Mexico, and the Mexican state of Chihuahua meet; a similar procession makes the pilgrimage during Easter week. Some hold candles, some crawl on their hands and knees as a sign of their religious devotion. It is the largest annual mass gathering on a Texas mountain.

FIELD NOTES: *Franklin Mountains and beyond. Trans Mountain Road, completed in 1969, swiftly climbs from the northeast side of El Paso, beyond the subdivisions, past the Border Patrol Museum and the boundary of the Castner Missile Range all the way to Smuggler's Pass, one mile above sea level. Clearing the pass, the mountains part and the view opens to the west. A swath of green bounds the narrow ribbon of the Rio Grande coursing through the low valley below. The river valley is a startling contrast to the barren desert that stretches to the next range, and the range after that, all the way to the horizon. Texas ends on the other side of the river, but the mountains—they never seem to quit.*

It's different out here.

Facing page
FRANKLIN MOUNTAINS
North Franklin Mountain

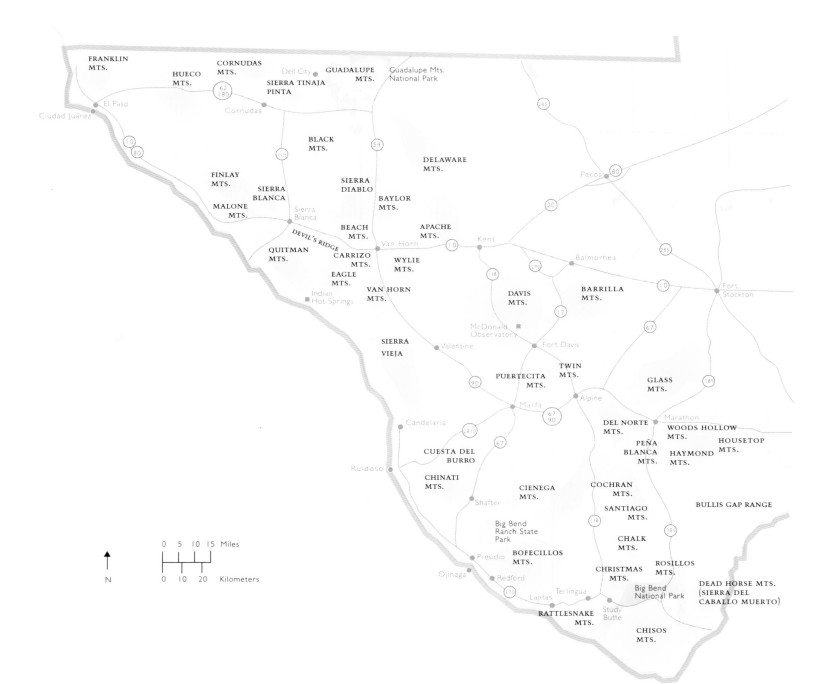

FRANKLIN
MTS.

HUECO
MTS.

CORNUDAS
MTS.

Dell City

GUADALUPE
MTS.

Guadalupe Mts.
National Park

SIERRA TINAJA
PINTA

El Paso

Ciudad Juárez

Cornudas

BLACK
MTS.

DELAWARE
MTS.

Pecos

FINLAY
MTS.

SIERRA
BLANCA

SIERRA
DIABLO

BAYLOR
MTS.

MALONE
MTS.

Sierra
Blanca

DEVIL'S RIDGE

BEACH
MTS.

APACHE
MTS.

Van Horn

Kent

Balmorhea

Fort
Stockton

QUITMAN
MTS.

CARRIZO
MTS.

WYLIE
MTS.

EAGLE
MTS.

VAN HORN
MTS.

DAVIS
MTS.

BARRILLA
MTS.

Indian
Hot Springs

SIERRA
VIEJA

McDonald
Observatory

Fort Davis

Valentine

PUERTECITA
MTS.

TWIN
MTS.

GLASS
MTS.

Marfa

Alpine

Candelaria

DEL NORTE
MTS.

Marathon

WOODS HOLLOW
MTS.

HOUSETOP
MTS.

CUESTA DEL
BURRO

PEÑA
BLANCA
MTS.

HAYMOND
MTS.

Ruidoso

CHINATI
MTS.

CIENEGA
MTS.

COCHRAN
MTS.

BULLIS GAP RANGE

Shafter

SANTIAGO
MTS.

Big Bend
Ranch State
Park

CHALK
MTS.

Presidio

BOFECILLOS
MTS.

ROSILLOS
MTS.

Ojinaga

Redford

CHRISTMAS
MTS.

Big Bend
National Park

DEAD HORSE MTS.
(SIERRA DEL
CABALLO MUERTO)

Lajitas

Terlingua

RATTLESNAKE
MTS.

Study
Butte

CHISOS
MTS.

0   5   10 15 Miles

0   10   20   Kilometers

N

There is no single, universally accepted source for elevations in mountain ranges. We have consulted the New Handbook of Texas *(Texas State Historical Association, 1996) and U.S. Geological Survey topographic maps of Far West Texas.*

APACHE MOUNTAINS

North and east of Van Horn, north and northwest of Kent. Approximately twenty miles long, northwest to southeast, a continuation of the Delawares to the northwest and the Davis Mountains to the southeast.

Highest elevation: 5,658 feet

One of three exposed portions of the largest fossil reef in the world (the other exposures are the Guadalupe and Glass mountains). Extremely dry, rocky slopes. Shallow, stony soils; oak, juniper, mesquite, piñon, and grasses.

BARRILLA MOUNTAINS

Eastern subrange of the Davis Mountains, extending almost thirty miles east from south-southeast of Balmorhea to northeast of Alpine.

Highest elevation: 5,568 feet

Desert mountain volcanic rock. Stony soils; grasses, madrone, live oak, piñon, juniper, maple, ponderosa pine.

Extensive pictographs in rock shelters. Source of springs at Balmorhea.

BAYLOR MOUNTAINS

Two miles north of Van Horn. Nine miles in length, north to south.

HIGHEST ELEVATION: 5,564 feet

Steep and rocky. Part of the same uplifted fault block as the Sierra Diablo and the Beach Mountains. Shallow, stony soils; grasses, oaks, live oaks, junipers, mesquites, piñon.

BEACH MOUNTAINS

Two miles northwest of Van Horn. Five miles in length, east to west.

Highest elevation: 5,933 feet

Steep and rocky; some of the oldest rocks (Precambrian) found in Texas Mountains. Shallow, stony soils; grasses, live oak, piñon, juniper. An intermediate range connecting the Sierra Diablo and the Baylor Mountains, all part of the western uplift bordering salt flats and the Delaware basin.

BLACK MOUNTAINS

Thirty miles northeast of Sierra Blanca. Four and a half miles long, east to west.

Highest elevation: 5,561 feet

Shallow, stony soils; scrub brush, grasses.

BOFECILLOS MOUNTAINS

Primary range of Big Bend Ranch State Park bordering the Rio Grande, extending forty-five miles from west-northwest of Big Bend National Park to northeast of Presidio.

Highest elevation: 5,135 feet (Oso Mountain)

Steep, rocky, loose rubble, largely sandstone, basalt, volcanic tuff. Dearth of soils; sparse grasses, cactus, scrub. More springs than nearby Chisos, microclimates around springs and waterfalls. Solitario collapsed caldera.

BAYLOR MOUNTAINS

CARRIZO MOUNTAINS
First light on mountain slopes

CARRIZO MOUNTAINS
Twenty-four miles southeast of Sierra Blanca and five miles west of Van Horn. Approximately five miles long, north to south.
Highest elevation: 5,304 feet (Carrizo Mountain)
Shallow, stony soils; scrub brush, creosote, cactus, mesquite, oak.
Precambrian rocks among oldest in the state.

CHINATI MOUNTAINS
Twenty-five miles south-southwest of Marfa, extending approximately fifteen miles north-northwest to southeast from Pinto Canyon to Cibolo Creek, thirty miles north of the Rio Grande.
Highest elevation: 7,728 feet (Chinati Peak)
Igneous origin, terraced and dissected mesas cut by steep canyons. Sparse, stony soils; grasses, cactus, scrub, scrub oaks. Forty-thousand-acre Chinati State Natural Area. Extensive silver mining in Shafter. Source for Chinati Hot Springs near Ruidosa.

CHISOS MOUNTAINS
Heart of Big Bend National Park, twenty miles in length southwest to northeast from Punta de la Sierra to Panther Junction.
Highest elevation: 7,835 feet (Emory Peak)
Most significant southern desert range in state. Dramatic steep slopes rising off desert floor. Shallow, stony soils; grasses, Texas madrone, and in high country and around springs, ponderosa pine, maple, Arizona cypress, aspen, Douglas fir.

CHRISTMAS MOUNTAINS
Twelve miles northeast of Terlingua on Terlingua Ranch, about five miles wide, west to east.
Highest elevation: 5,728 feet
Harsh, sparsely vegetated slopes. Shallow, stony soils; grasses, cactus, scrub, mesquite, juniper, oak.

CIENEGA MOUNTAINS
Nine miles east-southeast of Shafter.
Highest elevation: 5,223 feet
Dry, rocky slopes. Alluvial deposits of rubble; cactus, scrub, sparse grasses, oaks, cottonwoods around springs.

COCHRAN MOUNTAINS
Between Santiago and Del Norte Mountains.
Highest elevation: 5,562 feet
Piñon pine, juniper, cactus, desert scrub.

CORNUDAS MOUNTAINS
Seventy miles east of El Paso extending twenty miles from the other side of the New Mexico state line east-southeast to just west of Dell City.
Highest elevation (in Texas): 7,023 feet (San Antonio Mountain)
Steep and rocky. Extremely dry. Some peaks volcanic origin. Shallow, stony soils; grasses and scrub brush. Two major springs in range went dry in the 1980s.

CUESTA DEL BURRO
Twenty-two miles southwest of Marfa.
Highest elevation: 6,057 feet
Hilly range of rhyolite and conglomerate rubble, cut by canyons, separated from the Chinati Mountains to the south and west by Pinto Canyon. Some grasses, cactus, scrub, oak, and juniper.

DAVIS MOUNTAINS
West and west-southwest of Fort Davis, southeast of Kent, and northeast of Valentine.
Highest elevation: 8,378 feet (Mount Livermore)
The "Texas Alps" and the second-highest range in the state, with four major peaks—Mount Livermore, Sawtooth (7,686 feet), Mount Locke (6,791 feet, highest public road in Texas), and Blue Mountain (7,286). McDonald Observatory, Indian Lodge, Prude Ranch, Scenic Loop, a solar farm, a windmill farm, and Kit Carson's initials, dated Christmas Day, 1839, carved into a huge boulder at the Rockpile.
Volcanic origin. Shallow, stony soils; lush high-country grasses, cactus, Texas madrone, oak, live oak, maple, Arizona cypress, ponderosa pine, southwestern white pine, aspen.

CHRISTMAS MOUNTAINS
East Corazones Peak

DAVIS MOUNTAINS
Agave plant and bigtooth maples

DELAWARE MOUNTAINS

South of Guadalupe Pass in northwest Culberson County, thirty-eight miles in length, northwest to southeast.

Highest elevation: 5,888 feet

Steep and rocky, long horizontal layers of limestone, sandstone, and shale. Extremely dry and very lightly vegetated. Shallow, stony soils; grasses, juniper, piñon, live oak in canyons and upper ridges. Part of the same uplift on eastern border of salt flats as the Apaches to the southeast.

DEL NORTE MOUNTAINS

Eight miles east of Alpine extending twenty-six miles to Del Norte Gap, nineteen miles southwest of Marathon.

Highest elevation: 6,868 feet (Cathedral Mountain)

The northern part of a chain of mountains between Alpine and Marathon and the Big Bend. Shallow, stony soils; grasses, mesquite, oak, juniper, Texas madrone, maple, Arizona cypress, ponderosa pine on higher slopes.

DEVIL'S RIDGE

Four miles south of Sierra Blanca, extending southeast ten miles.

Highest elevation: 5,342 feet (Yucca Mesa)

Single ridge paralleling Quitman Mountains to southwest.

Sandy loams; grasses, scrub, some hardwoods on ridgetop.

EAGLE MOUNTAINS

Fifteen miles west-southwest of Van Horn and twenty-four miles south-southeast of Sierra Blanca, extending northwest to southeast fifteen miles.

Highest elevation: 7,484 feet (Eagle Mountain)

Rugged massif with several box canyons paralleling Interstate Highway 10 and the Southern Pacific rail route to the north. Shallow, stony soils; grasses, and cactus, and in canyons and high country, Texas madrone, bigtooth maple, juniper, piñon pine.

FINLAY MOUNTAINS

South central Hudspeth County, approximately ten miles west-northwest of Sierra Blanca. Seven miles in length, east to west.

Highest elevation: 5,710 feet

Steep, rocky slopes. Shallow, stony soils, sandy and clay loams; grasses, juniper, piñon, live oak.

FINLAY MOUNTAINS
Mountains and foothills

FRANKLIN MOUNTAINS

Texas's westernmost range, almost entirely surrounded by the city of El Paso, extending twenty miles north from just north of downtown to the New Mexico state line.

Highest elevation: 7,192 feet (North Franklin Mountain)

Steep and rocky. Very shallow, stony soils support grasses and scrub, some oaks around springs. Upper slopes are protected as part of Franklin Mountains State Park, the largest urban wilderness in the United States; otherwise almost completely surrounded by city.

GLASS MOUNTAINS

Easternmost major range in Texas, extending southwest to northeast fifty miles from ten miles east of Alpine to Monument Draw south of Fort Stockton.

Highest elevation: 6,520 feet

Low to steep and rocky. Like the Guadalupes and Apaches, exposed part of the largest limestone reef system in the world. Shallow, stony soils; grasses, mesquite, oak, juniper, piñon in higher elevations. Elk abundant. Source for Comanche Springs in Fort Stockton, the largest springs in West Texas until diesel pumping in 1950s caused flow to cease.

GUADALUPE MOUNTAINS

Most of fifty-mile range in southern New Mexico; southernmost and highest portion in northwestern Culberson County, 100 miles east of El Paso and about 25 miles east of Dell City.

Highest elevation: 8,749 feet (Guadalupe Peak, the highest mountain in Texas). Bush Mountain (8,631 feet), Shumard Peak (8,615 feet), and Bartlett Peak (8,508 feet) are the second, third, and fourth highest in the state. El Capitan (8,085 feet), at the southern tip of the range, is one of the most famous peaks in the southwestern United States.

Along with the Glass and Apache mountains, the Guadalupes are part of the Capitan Reef, a 400-mile-long horseshoe of hard limestone formed at the edge of the Delaware basin of the Permian Sea, 220 million to 280 million years ago. All of the range within Texas is part of the 86,415-acre Guadalupe Mountains National Park, which opened in September 1972.

Shallow, stony soils; grasses, scrub, cactus, and in high country and around springs in McKittrick Canyon, oak, ash, Texas madrone, bigtooth maple, alligator juniper, piñon pine, ponderosa, southwestern white pine, Douglas fir, aspen.

GLASS MOUNTAINS

HAYMOND MOUNTAINS

Thirteen miles southeast of Marathon, narrow chain no more than one mile wide and about four miles in length running northeast to southwest, southwest of House-top Mountains and due west of Peña Blanca Mountains.

Highest elevation: 4,180 feet

Part of the same chain as Woods Hollow and Peña Blanca mountains.

Shallow, stony, clay, and sandy loams; grasses, mesquite, live oak.

HOUSETOP MOUNTAINS

Eighteen miles southeast of Marathon, four miles long, extending northwest to southeast.

Highest elevation: 5,460 feet

Long, narrow ridge. First legitimate mountains on westbound U.S. Highway 90. Fine, sandy loams; grasses, brush, hardwoods, piñon pine, juniper.

HUECO MOUNTAINS

Thirty-five miles east-northeast of El Paso. Approximately twenty miles in length from north (the New Mexico state line) to south-southeast.

Highest elevation: 6,787 feet (Cerro Alto)

Shallow, stony soils; oak, juniper, scrub brush and grasses. Abundant natural basins, or Hueco tanks, dependable water source. Exceptional rock art. Considered one of two best in the world for bouldering.

MALONE MOUNTAINS

Ten miles west of Sierra Blanca, extending six miles to northwest.

Highest elevation: 5,062 feet

Rocky slopes. Shallow, stony soils, sandy and clay loams; grasses, cactus, scrub, juniper, live oak.

PEÑA BLANCA MOUNTAINS

Nine miles southeast of Marathon. Five miles long, northeast to southwest.

Highest elevation: 4,550 feet

Shallow, stony soils; scrub brush, mesquite, creosote, cactus, grasses; and juniper in the higher areas.

PUERTECITA MOUNTAINS

Ten miles south of Fort Davis.

Highest elevation: 6,285 feet

A single mountain more than a range. Shallow, stony soils; grasses, madrone, ponderosa pine, maple, piñon pine, oak, juniper.

QUITMAN MOUNTAINS

Seven miles west of Sierra Blanca, extending twenty-four miles southwest.

Highest elevation: 6,681 feet

Shallow, stony soils, some clay and sandy loams; grasses, live oak, juniper, piñon; madrone, maple on higher ridges. The most formidable landmass barrier to east-west transportation routes in Far West Texas.

RATTLESNAKE MOUNTAINS

Circular desert range just west of Big Bend National Park along Terlingua Creek.

Highest elevation: 2,911 feet, lowest recognized range in state

Largely rubble, volcanic in origin. Virtually no soils; desert scrub

ROSILLOS MOUNTAINS

Nine miles north of Panther Junction and Big Bend National Park, circular range some seven miles in diameter, between Santiago Mountains and Sierra del Caballo Muerto.

Highest elevation: 5,445 feet (Rosillos Peak)

Part of intrusive igneous mass. Shallow, stony soils; grasses, juniper, and scrub brush.

SANTIAGO MOUNTAINS

Twenty-four miles south-southwest of Marathon and extending thirty-two miles in length northwest to southeast to Persimmon Gap in Big Bend National Park.

Highest elevation: 6,524 feet (Santiago Peak)

Shallow, stony soils; mesquite, oak, juniper, and piñon pine.

DEVIL'S RIDGE

SIERRA BLANCA

Two miles north of Sierra Blanca, ten miles in length, stretching to the northwest.

Highest elevation: 6,890 feet (Sierra Blanca Peak)

Three conical volcanic peaks, the largest, Sierra Blanca Peak, a regional landmark visible from El Paso, Van Horn, and the Guadalupes. Clay and sandy loams; grasses, cactus, scrub.

SIERRA DEL CABALLO MUERTO, DEAD HORSE MOUNTAINS

Fifteen miles southeast of Persimmon Gap in Big Bend National Park, thirty miles in length from southeastern Brewster County to the Rio Grande.

Highest elevation: 5,854 feet (Sue Peaks)

Continuation of Santiagos and subrange of the Sierra del Carmen that rises above 9,000 feet in Coahuila, Mexico, whose southernmost portion forms north wall of Boquillas Canyon, longest of three canyons in Big Bend National Park.

Extremely barren, rocky slopes, cut by dry washes and shut-ins. Shallow, stony soils. Scrub, cactus; mesquite, desert willows in canyons and arroyos.

SIERRA DIABLO

Twelve miles northwest of Van Horn and twelve miles northeast of Sierra Blanca, extending nineteen miles north-northeast, roughly paralleling Texas Highway 54.

Highest elevation: 6,610 feet

Extremely rugged, uninhabited cuesta ridge, gently rising from west to east and dramatically dropping east from ridgeline. Western flank of Delaware basin. Shallow, stony soils; grasses, cactus, mesquite, oak, piñon, and in canyons and on ridgeline, Texas madrone, bigtooth maple.

SIERRA TINAJA PINTA

Thirteen miles southwest of Dell City and four miles northeast of Cornudas.

Highest elevation: 5,717 feet

Series of igneous extrusion hills, approximately thirty-five million years old. Steep, rocky slopes. Very shallow, stony soils; grasses, scrub, live oak, piñon, juniper.

SIERRA VIEJA

Forty-two miles northwest of Marfa extending sixteen miles south from Van Horn Mountains to Chinati Mountains.

Highest elevation: 6,500 feet (Vieja Peak)

Almost contiguous ridge of igneous origin. Shallow, stony soils; grasses, cactus, oaks, juniper, piñon, maples on ridge and around springs.

TWIN MOUNTAINS

Twelve miles southeast of Fort Davis.

Highest elevation: 6,895 feet

A connected pair of high peaks. Part of the Davis Mountains complex. Piñon pine, oak, juniper, and grasses.

VAN HORN MOUNTAINS

Nine miles southwest of Van Horn, extending sixteen miles southeast, between Sierra Vieja and Eagle Mountains.

Highest elevation: 5,640 feet

Rugged, rocky slopes. Shallow, stony soils; grasses, cactus, scrub, juniper, piñon, live oak.

WOODS HOLLOW MOUNTAINS

Four miles southeast of Marathon. Eight miles long, southwest to northeast.

Highest elevation: 4,661 feet

Part of the main chain of mountains between Marathon and Big Bend National Park, east of U.S. Highway 385. Shallow, stony soils, and calcareous clays; cactus, grasses, mesquite, live oak, and juniper in higher areas.

WYLIE MOUNTAINS

Four miles southeast of Van Horn. Seven miles in length, northwest to southeast.

Highest elevation: 5,310 feet

Steep and rocky, uplifted block of Permian carbonate. Shallow, stony soils; grasses, mesquite, oak, juniper, piñon.

ACKNOWLEDGMENTS

*M*any people helped both of us with this book—allowing access to their land, offering places to stay, making introductions, and providing many other indispensable favors.

TOGETHER we wish to thank Bruce Blakemore, Mike Bradford, Jerri Bramblett, Dolph Briscoe, Mike and Anne Capron, Tana Christie, Dan Damon, Laura and Chris Gill, Ann Gillespie, Jerry Hall, Larry Henderson, Ty Hunt, Bruce Jackson, Bobby and Pat Jones, John Karges, Steve and Carla Kennedy, Tony Kunitz, Mike Long, Euraline McVay, Crawford Marginot, Clay and Jodie Miller, Fred and Ernestina Nelan, Debbie and Mike O'Neill, Susan Potts, Harwood Puett, Nelson Puett, John Sanders, Andy Sansom, Hiram Sibley, Jane Sibley, Ray Sierra, Lloyd and Mattie Stuessy, Joe and Sharon Tammen, David and Jennifer Whitesell, Russell Wilbanks, and Trey Woodward.

LAURENCE PARENT also wishes to thank David Alloway, Luis Armendariz, Kit Bramblett, Joe Christie, Boyd Elder, George Fore, Mary Foster, Charles King, James King, Darice McVay, Pilar Ortega, Patricia Caperton Parent, and James Schilling.

JOE NICK PATOSKI wishes to thank in particular Lisa and Artie Ahier, Val Beard, Gorden Bell, Jim Bones, Jake Brisbin, Catfish Calloway, David Courtney, Lynn Crittendon, Susan and Tom Curry, Gregory Curtis, Mike Davidson, Tom Diamond, Bob Dillard, Joseph Fitzsimons, Larry Francell, Beth Garcia, Kiko Garcia, Butch Hancock, David and Holly Hollingsworth, Todd Jagger, Luis Jimenez, Don Kennard, Tammy King, Mike Levy, Gene Lutrick, Jim Lynch, Malcolm McGregor, Jan McInroy, Jack and Bonnie McNamara, Betty Moore, Gary Oliver, Carlos Ramirez, Ellis Richard, Tom Russell, Benjamin Saenz, Marc Schwartz, Evan Smith, Teresa Todd, and Jim White.

DELAWARE MOUNTAINS
Thunderstorm over Delaware and distant
Guadalupe mountains

TEXAS MOUNTAINS

Design and typography by
Teresa W. Wingfield
for the University of Texas Press

Text: 9.5 on 14 Trump Mediaeval
and display: Diotima

Set in Pagemaker 6.5
on a Power Macintosh system

Printed and bound by
Regent Publishing Services, Ltd.

Printed on
157 gsm Mitsubishi Matte Art Paper